BAREFOOT IN ATHENS

Maxwell Anderson

Barefoot
in Athens

WILLIAM SLOANE ASSOCIATES, INC.

PUBLISHERS   NEW YORK

PRINTED IN THE UNITED STATES
AT THE COUNTRY LIFE PRESS, GARDEN CITY, N.Y.

For Mab

Socrates and His Gospel

Socrates was put to death in Athens in 399 B.C. Nothing had been written about him during his life except *The Clouds*, a caricature for the comic stage, but after his death a whole school of writing grew up around him. Socratic dialogues were written by at least seven men whose names we know, and probably by many others. It was all the rage to write these question-and-answer scenes with Socrates as the central character, much as the sonnet sequence was all the rage in the England of 1590.

Some of the men who wrote the dialogues had been students or companions of Socrates. No doubt they tried to give a fairly accurate account of their dead master. Knowing, however, that there was no shorthand system in those days, we can be sure that neither the exact words of Socrates nor the exact order of events was ever recorded. It was probably not considered important that the record be exact. Each man, writing a dialogue, was turning out his own work of art and taking certain liberties with his recollection, even when he was not constructing an imaginary conversation which he thought Socrates might have had. It is instructive that the two accounts of Socrates' trial that remain agree in only one passage, the wording of the indictment. Socrates is quoted at length in both, but there are few even roughly parallel arguments, and none identical.

Time has destroyed the great mass of dialogues which was written after Socrates' death and has saved only the work of two men—Xenophon and Plato. Both had spent much time with Socrates, both were young when he died, both lived to old age and wrote extensively. Both were gifted enough to make a place in world literature, but Xenophon is known as a minor historian, Plato as a master thinker. In their own day they seem not to have been friends. Xenophon's letters are critical of Plato's portrait of Socrates, and Xenophon was doubtful about showing his own dialogues beyond a circle of intimates, fearing to detract from Socrates' reputation by faulty reporting. He was obviously of the opinion that Plato had reported Socrates incorrectly and had damaged his name and fame. Naturally he could not know that Plato's name and fame would brighten during the coming twenty-four centuries till they almost extinguished Socrates. Plato was a powerful and unique literary artist and the power of perfect literary expression is beyond that of any military conqueror. Plato took over Socrates, wiped out Xenophon (with many others), inspired Aristotle and became the leading philospher of the western world.

When I studied Plato at the University of North Dakota under Professor Hult, a learned and lovable man, there was no doubt in his mind that Plato was as scrupulously honest as he was great. There is still no doubt of his greatness. His dialogues carry over into every translation an atmosphere like that of Athens—brilliant without flash, colorful without heaviness, heady without intoxication. He makes his points so skillfully, he designs his scenes so well, that he often seems to be making no point, to have no design. Yet there is a point always, and a design too; the reader has been led along an enchanting path to a carefully chosen conclusion, whether he is aware of it or not.

Early in this century the name of Plato was always associated, in academic circles, with heavenly sweetness, pure intent, and a laudable longing for the golden age among men. I was somewhat chilled, myself, on first reading *The Republic*, to discover that the rulers of Plato's ideal state took stern charge of the arts, allowing only certain martial modes of music and throwing out the poets and romancers altogether. However, nobody else seemed to object and it was an old quarrel, so I thought little of the matter. I continued to read the early dialogues, in which Socrates' ideas were completely democratic, and to let *The Republic* and *The Laws* severely alone.

More and more, as I grew older, I was troubled in reading Plato by discovering that I did not like the Socrates who continued to discourse so charmingly and so bewilderingly in the later dialogues. I didn't like him because I didn't trust him. I caught him playing tricks with words, not for fun, and not to get at the truth, but to conceal and throw dust and obfuscate. I distrusted my mistrust at first, for I had grown up reverencing the founder of the first academy and went to him in search of wisdom, not to criticize. But after the second world-wide war, when communism and military aggression became obvious partners, I went back to Plato to unearth what he had been getting at in his *Republic*, and what relation his utopia might have to modern times. In order to be sure of what *The Republic* meant I had to read the other dialogues, and while doing this I discovered that the editors and scholars and translators had definite ideas about the order in which Plato's works were written. Some of the evidence was exterior and conclusive. It is known, for example, that *The Laws* is Plato's last work. It is fairly well established that *The Apology* was the first in which Socrates' name was used, and that *Crito* was written at about the same time. Given these beginning and ending dates it is possible to fix without much doubt the order of the whole series, for Plato traveled a single track in his thinking and he made a long journey. He went all the way from individualism and democracy in *The Apology* to a communistic and brutal dictatorship in *The Laws*, and each dialogue marks a station along this melancholy path.

When you examine Plato's *Republic* you find that he is not describing a republic at all, but a dictatorship. It contains two classes, the rulers or warriors, who are armed, and the ruled or workers, who are not armed. The armed rulers are superior to the unarmed workers in three ways—in race, in education, and in moral values. Methods of breeding and training the rulers are carefully worked out. There is to be no changing over from one class to another. There is to be no change at all after the pattern of the state is once fixed. It is to function, we must presume, like the civilization of the bees, in which life and hive patterns are repeated like a rite by every new generation, and any innovation or novel thought or criticism would be punished by death.

It is true that Plato describes his utopia as an ancient form of government, the archetype from which nations have fallen away to modern degenerate makeshifts. But he passionately contends that we must find our way back to it, and that men will never be well governed while they have to choose among the existing political orders—kingdoms, tyrannies (of the one, the few, or the many), and democracies. He is most violently opposed to democracy, turning his full battery of scurrilous abuse on government by the people. The people when in power are said in *The Republic* to be prodigal and miserly, unscrupulous, over-bearing, shameless, without law, as insatiable as sharks and beasts of prey, living only for pleasure and the gratification of unclean desires. When the people are in power "reverence is folly, temperance is cowardice, moderation and the keeping of accounts is meanness." "But the crest of this wild wave of freedom is reached," Plato makes Socrates say, "when male and female slaves, bought and paid for, are allowed as much liberty as those who own them. . . . And what is the end result of all this? People's hearts are so wrung by the sight of men and women in bondage that they advocate the manumission of all slaves and believe slavery to be an evil, even when the slave is treated well." Plato gave his voice unequivocally to slavery.

And how are the workers to be held under control in Plato's republic? There is to be an official doctrine concerning everything, and this doctrine must be believed throughout the state. Does this doctrine include lies? Yes, Plato is honest about that. A certain amount of official lying must be decided upon and promulgated by the rulers. What then is to happen to any stubborn men who refuse to think and act as the rulers wish? This also Plato answers directly. A special nocturnal court must be set up to deal with such cases. Pressure will be used, and if it is unsuccessful the rebellious citizen will be quietly put away. Liquidation is a modern word in this connection, but it is a fair translation of what Plato proposes to do with recalcitrants. No doubt Plato set out to define a happy society in his republic, but what we find in his pages, if we boil it down, is something very much like Russia under the Politburo. Marx, too, intended a happy society when he planned his utopia. Maybe utopia always turns out this way. But to put such doctrines in the mouth of Socrates is a betrayal as deliberate as Alcibiades' betrayal of Athens. Having written honestly about Socrates in *Crito* and *The Apology*, Plato began to fudge and side-step and prevaricate as his own opinions altered. And these new beliefs of his were attributed to Socrates in all the later dialogues except *The Laws*. In this last dialogue even the name of Socrates is discarded and Plato states his final communist doctrine. The style is charming, the content repulsive.

THE THREE GOSPELS

Turning to Xenophon's *Memorabilia* one enters another world, containing an entirely different Socrates. Xenophon was a soldier, a country gentleman, a hunter, a historian, an expert horseman, and a competent reporter. When he wrote about Socrates it was not to expound his own ideas, for he had none, it was to defend the Socrates he had known against the calumny of those who had procured his death and those who still went about blackening the name of his former master. Xenophon knew that he was not a literary genius and he suspected that Plato was. Nevertheless he was scornful of Plato's "love of tyrants, and preferring the luxury of a Sicilian table before a frugal life." Plato visited both the first and the second Dionysius and tried unsuccessfully to work out an ideal state with each of them. How frugal Xenophon's life may have been we don't know. We do know from his letters that he kept up his friendship with Socrates' old friends, Crito and Phaedo, and that he contributed to the support of Socrates' wife and children after his death.

But a good heart is not essential to the equipment of genius, and some of nature's noblemen have been dull fellows. Xenophon wrote well, sometimes excitingly, as in the description of the first sight of the sea in the *Anabasis*, but his dialogues have only a faint touch of the electric atmosphere we feel as we read Plato. His *Banquet* is no match for the *Symposium*, his account of the trial no match for *The Apology*. *Crito* and *The Apology* have, by their sheer artistry, written Socrates' character and thought in flame across our western skies. Without them the world would have found Socrates, as he is in Xenophon, a wise old fellow, but nobody's pillar of fire.

For myself I shall always thank Plato for writing truly, movingly, and gloriously about Socrates in his youth, and shall thank Xenophon for proving to me that what Plato put into Socrates' mouth in his middle and old age was largely lies. The gospels that relate the life and sayings of Socrates are really three. First, the gospel according to the young Plato, when he still held to the democratic opinions of Pericles and Socrates. Second, the gospel according to the older Plato, after he had become Socrates' Judas and turned against him and Athens. Third, the gospel according to Xenophon, a good, unimaginative reporter, whose descriptions of his master are factual and as accurate as he could make them, but never do bring the man alive. I omit *The Clouds*, which might make a fourth, because it is obviously a burlesque.

HOW DID IT HAPPEN?

And how did it come about that Plato betrayed his beloved master? I have one purely personal theory. Plato was twenty-three when Athens called for Socrates' execution. Up to this time Plato had taken democracy for granted and liked its ways. Suddenly and tragically he lost the great man who was closest to his heart; he was young; he turned against the rabble (or what seemed to him rabble) of Athens. He turned against democracy and tried to work out a new kind of government in which philosophers would not run the danger of being killed by inferior people who did not like their views. He tried to work it out on paper and he tried to work it out among men—as witness his attempts with the Dionysius dynasty in Sicily. He became convinced that one-man rule was not the answer, just as the rule of the many was not the answer. He found himself coming closer and closer in his thinking to the communism of Sparta, making only one significant change from it in the utopia he imagined—the upper class, the ruling class, must consist not of a hereditary hierarchy of stupidity, they must be philosopher-kings. How they were to be chosen he left somewhat vague, perhaps unable to make up his own mind. And this is the central question, the question that bedevils the whole earth. There has never been a good way to train, test, or choose the holders of political power. The democratic—or republican—method is the best we know; though it's not too admirable, with its local and national bosses, its inevitable spoils system, its routine corruption. The communist system, with its gang of assassins in office, is the worst we know. Plato was sufficiently astute to see that the rigid structure of a communist society could be maintained only by a ruthless use of assassination, yet he chucked democracy and came out for communism. At least his philosopher-kings, once chosen, would that way be safe from the mob.

THE WORLD THEY LIVED IN

Our age is not the first which has seen democracy and communism in open conflict. The latter half of the life of Socrates was lived during a long quarrel between a communist state and a democratic state. Sparta was a complete, thorough and conscious communist society. Athens was the first conscious attempt at a democracy.

Sparta was a closed, hard, grim slave state, in which the men and women lived in separate barracks and the children were appropriated and indoctrinated by the authorities as soon as the mother's milk was out of them. Sparta had neither commerce nor art, and nothing has come down to us from that stolid city except a fable about a boy who allowed his entrails to be eaten by a fox rather than cry out. No vase, no sculpture, no architecture, no literature was produced by Sparta in the great period of the Greeks.

Athens, a commercial city, trading by land and sea, during the same period invented democracy, named it, defined it, and turned loose a flood of creative work in every field that has set the pace for western civilization ever since. Her theater, her architecture, her sculpture, her science, and her philosophy made brilliant patterns for all later cultures and nations. Not till the Renaissance was comparable work done in the arts, and even then the creators and craftsmen looked back to the Mediterranean society founded by Athens for their models.

These startling achievements of the Athens which Socrates knew have blinded many scholars to the imperfections of her political structure. To us it would seem a mockery to call a city a democracy when the vast majority of its inhabitants were slaves, yet this was the case in Athens. An empire is essentially undemocratic, yet Athens held an empire. It was an indefensible law which required that a citizen of Athens must be able to point both to an Athenian father and an Athenian mother. The courts of Athens, growing raggedly and without plan out of the old aristocratic councils, consisted of huge paid juries (quite often of five hundred) with only a cloudy concept of what the law might be and a liking for flowery and misleading oratory. These juries seem to have been asked many times to pass on whether or not the defendant was a good fellow rather than on his guilt or innocence. Quite often, too, the jury was asked to decide what the law might be as well as on whether or not the defendant had broken it. Trials frequently had the appearance of amusements staged for the entertainment of the jury rather than inquiries into the truth or falsity of a charge.

The trial of Socrates had some of this character. He had begun as a sort of Will Rogers of the market place, homely, witty, unbeatable in argument, afraid of nobody, too shrewd to make enemies, too honest to make powerful friends. As he grew older he became the accepted critic of Athenian institutions. He invented a question-and-answer game which he played with such skill that it seems to have ended almost invariably with his antagonist impaled on a verbal spit. The young-men-about-town began to keep him company for the fun of these sessions, and some of them became his followers and disciples.

Some, unfortunately, like Alcibiades, Critias, and Charmides, enjoyed his company and his dialectics for a while and then, perhaps out of ambition, perhaps made cynical by Socrates' attacks on power politics and the intellectual dishonesty of statesmen, turned against democracy and against Athens. They were perilously clever men, these three, and when they became unscrupulous they were dangerous enemies. They sold out to Persia or to

Sparta or to whatever enemy offered most, and before they had done with their treasons Sparta, with the help of Persia, had conquered Athens. For a brief bitter time there were Spartan troops on the Acropolis and the traitor, Critias, governed Athens under Spartan direction. When the Spartans were driven out and the democracy had been restored one of its first acts was to put Socrates on trial. He was accused by three leading citizens of not worshiping the gods, of introducing new deities of his own, and of corrupting the young men of the city. The young men alluded to were Alcibiades, Critias, and Charmides—and the indictment was based on a complete misunderstanding of Socrates' motives.

He criticized his city because he loved it and wanted to keep it in line, not because he wanted to destroy it or even to change it in any fundamental fashion. To his way of life and his way of thought democracy was an absolute essential. But when he was tried the jury considered the evidence against him, considered his own casual, independent defense, and decided by a rather close vote, that he was guilty as charged. It was probably not expected that this would be a death sentence, for in cases of this sort the defendant was usually given a chance at a lighter penalty— exile, or a fine, or, in some instances, escape to another city.

But an unexpected difficulty arose. In order that he get off with a lighter punishment than death Socrates would have had to admit that he had been a destructive force in Athens. He could not honestly admit this because he did not believe it. Rather than say what he did not believe he preferred to die. And he pointed out humorously to his accusers that it would be a very bad thing for Athens if he died, because it would give Athens a bad name, but a good thing for him because it would make his name remembered.

Nevertheless, the verdict stood. The jury could not change its vote without losing face, and Socrates went to prison. He was then given an opportunity to escape, but again a difficulty presented itself. Socrates did not wish to be disloyal to Athens, even to the extent of escaping from her jurisdiction. He had fought against the verdict but once it became a fact he accepted it and would not revolt against it by running away.

Also there was no other democracy in the world at that time. If Socrates had run to any other city around the rim of the known world—the Mediterranean—he would have encountered despotism in one form or another—the kings of the Orient, the tyrants of Sicily, southern Italy, or northern Africa—or the even more repressive communist despotism of Sparta. There was no life for him in any of these unfree places. He stayed in prison and drank the poison when the jailer brought it.

And Plato, in his lifelong desperate search for the state that would shelter philosophers, overlooked the state that had produced Socrates and himself. Things came about as Socrates had anticipated—his death made him famous, made his city infamous. Yet if he had been executed in Sparta, where injustice was erected into a system, his death would have passed unnoticed. It was because Athens made an attempt at justice that this outstanding miscarriage of justice had so stunning an effect not only on Plato but on the world. If there arose a great philosopher in Russia today (supposing this possible), and he were put out of the way because his sayings became an offense to the authorities, no record of his sayings or his trial or his death would ever see the light. If Socrates had lived and died in Sparta (supposing this possible), he would never have been heard of by the world outside, nor could Plato, had he lived in Sparta, have written any of his books except perhaps *The Laws*.

XENOPHON AND XANTIPPE

Xantippe is so exclusively known as a shrew that some readers of *Barefoot in Athens* may question the accuracy of the portrait I draw of her there. Naturally I know no more about Xantippe's home life than does anybody else, but a letter from Xenophon to Xantippe, written after Socrates' death, exists and gives a hint of Xantippe's character which seems to contradict the legend. I quote the letter in full:

FROM XENOPHON IN MEGARA
TO XANTIPPE IN ATHENS

"I am sending you six measures of meal, eight drachmas, and a new garment for the coming winter. They will be brought by Euphron of Megara. Accept them, please, and take my word that Euclid and Terpsion are good and honest persons who always had a great affection for you and Socrates. If your sons wish to visit me here do not forbid it, for the journey to Megara is neither long nor difficult.

"Pray do not weep any more. It may do harm and it cannot help. Remember what Socrates said. Follow his practice and precepts. Further grieving will but wrong yourself and your children. They are the children of Socrates, and we are obligated not only to care for them but to care for ourselves for their sake. For if you or I or anyone who ought to look after them should fail now the children of Socrates might be left unprotected. I myself study to live for them, and you will not live unless you take care of yourself. Grief is the enemy of life, for it favors death.

"Apollodorus and Dion speak well of you, reporting that you refuse to accept gifts and give as your reason that you are rich and have no need of charity. This is well done. As long as I and other friends have anything you shall not want. Be of good courage, Xantippe, and lose nothing of Socrates. Knowing how great he was, think of his life, not of his death. Still, the death, too, if you consider it carefully, appears noble and excellent. Farewell."

BAREFOOT IN ATHENS

Act One

Barefoot in Athens

Act One

SCENE I

SCENE: *It's near the end of the fifth century B.C. in Athens, and we are in the house of Socrates indicated by props, not sets.* XANTIPPE, *Socrates' wife, is setting some breakfast before their three sons, meanwhile talking to Socrates in the next room and to the boys also. The eldest, Lamprocles, is eighteen or more, the second son, Lysis, is eleven or twelve, the third, little Phoenix, is a youngster.*

XANTIPPE You may as well eat. We have no truck with etiquette in this house. He'll come to breakfast when he's thought it all over.

LAMPROC. He's thinking of shaving. Somebody made him a present of a bronze razor.

XANTIPPE Shaving!

LYSIS You think he will?

LAMPROC. Well, why not?

LYSIS I hope he does.

1

XANTIPPE Why?

LYSIS I just hope he does.

XANTIPPE I hope he doesn't. Socrates?

SOCRATES [*Off stage*] Yes, Xantippe?

XANTIPPE Are you shaving?

SOCRATES [*Off stage*] I'm thinking of it. I'm trying the edge on a few stray hairs.

XANTIPPE Leave it the way it is. At least part of your face is covered.

LYSIS At the field they—ah—

XANTIPPE Yes?

LYSIS For a long while they didn't know he was my father. They made fun of his bare feet and his funny whiskers—and I didn't say anything. But now they know and . . .
[SOCRATES *enters*]
Aren't you going to shave, father?

SOCRATES I decided against it. Fear of the unknown, I suppose. Who knows what's underneath? It might be worse.

[*He sits*]

XANTIPPE That's optimism. But it certainly wouldn't do any harm for you to trim your beard, and to wear sandals and proper clothes. Still, it's no good talking. You'll do as you've always done.
[*She touches his shoulder*]
Your robe's unpinned.

SOCRATES [*Rising to adjust it*] By the dog, if this civilization of ours is ever dug up, or leaves any pictures of itself, we'll cut a comic figure in history! Look at this fantastic rig we wear—look at this chiton or himation or whatever it is—

XANTIPPE It's been both in its time, and it's neither now.

SOCRATES Well, look at it—it doesn't keep you warm in winter, it
doesn't keep you cool in summer, it doesn't shed rain, it
doesn't turn wind; it hobbles you when you walk, it trips
you up when you run, and it ties you in knots when you fall
down!

XANTIPPE A new one would be simpler to fasten, but you'd manage to
look comical in anything you wore, I've learned that.

SOCRATES Is there money for a new one?

XANTIPPE Not unless you brought money home with you last night.

SOCRATES That's what I forgot! Simmias owes me ten drachmas on an
old debt, but we stood so long talking about the war that I
forgot to ask for it.

XANTIPPE Ten drachmas! That's a fortune! And you forgot it!

SOCRATES Let's not be loose in our thinking, my dear. What's your
definition of a fortune?

XANTIPPE Any amount that takes a load off your mind! Any amount in
excess of two obols, which is what we have in the house at
present! I was about to send Lamprocles to the market to
buy a fish with one obol. The other—I suppose we could
just throw it around.

LAMPROC. [Rising] Father?

SOCRATES Yes, Lamprocles.

LAMPROC. If you have that much money . . . there's a contingent of
heavy-armed foot soldiers leaving for the south tomorrow.
I'm all trained and ready, and if I had three drachmas to
buy a sword and shield I could go with them.

SOCRATES Could you buy a sword and shield for three drachmas?

LAMPROC. They've been used, but they're in good shape.

XANTIPPE They're in better shape than the soldier who used them, I'm certain of that.

SOCRATES The truth is, Simmias sails with supplies for the fleet this morning, and he's probably already gone.

LAMPROC. Oh.
[*He sits*]
There go the ten drachmas.

XANTIPPE Well, for once I thank Zeus for our poverty! Why would you want to go with the army?

LAMPROC. To fight for Athens.

XANTIPPE You're not old enough!

LAMPROC. I'm exactly the age they're asking for.

XANTIPPE If you had any brains you'd stay out of it.

LAMPROC. My father fought for Athens.

XANTIPPE I know—the famous barefoot campaign—barefoot he fought, barefoot he won—the others were freezing all about him, but he marched sturdily on over ice and snow in his one ragged garment, filling his comrades with courage and the enemy with despair. And what did we get out of it? The war's still going on. It's been going on twenty-six years and we're twenty-six times worse off now than we were when it started—

LAMPROC. But we can't stop!

XANTIPPE You've been stopped by your father's improvidence, and a lucky thing, too. It's best to go early for the fish, while there's plenty to choose from.

[*She finds a copper in her leather purse and hands it to him*]

LAMPROC. Very well.

SOCRATES I'm sorry, son.

LAMPROC. It doesn't matter. I'll find the money sooner or later.

[*He goes out.* SOCRATES *takes a bite*]

XANTIPPE Would you let him go into the war?

SOCRATES Strangely enough, I find that I don't want him to go. Yet I allowed myself to go, and other young men are going. It's a problem.

XANTIPPE This is our son, our son, Socrates! Will you quit thinking of everything as a problem and come to some conclusion?

SOCRATES Sometimes I think the earth is not well equipped with conclusions.

XANTIPPE In the name of Pallas Athena, what does that mean?

SOCRATES What it says—that nothing is decided, nothing ever concluded, nothing comes to an end.

XANTIPPE Men come to an end in battle!

SOCRATES Yes, that's the nearest there is to an end, and it turns out to be a beginning.

XANTIPPE If there's anything more infuriating than words it's more words!

SOCRATES Let's be silent.

[*They eat*]

LYSIS Father?

SOCRATES Yes?

LYSIS You know those sandals that Alcibiades gave you for a joke one time?

SOCRATES I know them very well. They still hang on my wall.

LYSIS   Do they fit you?

SOCRATES   They look as if they would.

LYSIS   Would you put them on . . . once a day . . . just for me?

SOCRATES   What is this you ask—once a day?

LYSIS   Father . . . when you walk down to the city in the morning you pass the athletic field where I am with the other boys of my age. And they laugh at you, because you don't wear shoes or sandals. Couldn't you put them on—and wear them when you pass the field—and then take them off?

SOCRATES   Lysis, my poor Lysis.

           [*He puts an arm around Lysis*]

LYSIS   Will you wear them?

SOCRATES   They'd laugh at me with or without sandals, Lysis.

LYSIS   Not so much with them.

SOCRATES   Lysis, are the boys happy when they laugh or unhappy?

LYSIS   Oh, they're happy, but I'm not.

SOCRATES   Then I cause great happiness by not wearing sandals!

LYSIS   [*Leaping from the table*] I tell you I can't go there any more if you're to pass by like that every morning and be laughed at! I tell you they laugh till they fall on the ground and roll! I can't stand it, and I can't go there, and I hate them and I hate you if you're going to be a laughing stock! You could put on the sandals just to go by and then take them off! You could—

           [*He breaks off and weeps*]

SOCRATES   The truth is, I couldn't put them on.

LYSIS   Yes you could! You just won't! It's some kind of silly pride!

SOCRATES   I thought perhaps it was pride, and I examined that—

LYSIS   Oh, you examined and you discussed—I know—and it came out your way!

SOCRATES   I'm afraid you're my most stubborn antagonist, son—next to your mother. But there is a way round this difficulty. I'll take the upper path when I walk down to the market, and they won't see me at all.

LYSIS   You will?

SOCRATES   Of course I will. I like a change of habits.

LYSIS   Will you go that way this morning?

SOCRATES   Indeed I will. They shan't see any trace of me—nose, belly, or feet.

LYSIS   That's—that's wonderful! It's late! I'll go now!

[*He runs out*]

PHOENIX   I want to play at the spring.

XANTIPPE   Don't stray beyond the plane tree.

PHOENIX   No, mother.

[*He goes out. She looks out after him, then returns to Socrates*]

XANTIPPE   We're at rock bottom, Socrates. We have one obol in the house and no prospect of more. . . . Socrates, when I married you I was madly in love with you.

SOCRATES   Well, I still exasperate you, Xantippe, so there's some affection left.

XANTIPPE   At any rate, I was madly in love and I brought you a little money. Not much, but I collect a little silver every quarter, and it used to be enough so that we could live, even when you brought nothing home. But the war goes on and on and money buys less and less, till now it's not enough. It's not half enough, and you must earn a little or we'll starve.

SOCRATES Those ten drachmas are due me for work done on the pillars of Simmias' house thirty years ago, when I was still a stone-cutter. I could work at that again.

XANTIPPE No, you couldn't. You could no more do that than you could wear sandals; but there's one thing you could do, you could take money for the lessons you give.

SOCRATES I give no lessons.

XANTIPPE You have a large following, and you are held in greater esteem than any other teacher in Athens. You are offered money by handfuls and you won't take it!
[*He lifts his hand*]
Be quiet! Let me finish: I know of at least six other teachers in Athens—Hippias, Prodicus, Gorgias, Polus, and Callicles—and every one of them is well paid, well dressed, well fed and solvent. And you could be!

SOCRATES If I took money for what I say I'd be cheating my listeners, for I truly know nothing. All I have is a kind of skill in argument—

XANTIPPE And that's what they go to you for! That's what they use you for! Alcibiades did it, and Critias, and dozens of others! These young men spend a few years with you, and suddenly they're great orators and powers in the state, while here you sit just as before, in the same old shirt and probably the same old dirt, because you've never been quite sure that bathing was good for people!

SOCRATES When you are searching for truth, my dear, money can only corrupt you. Once get into the habit of taking it and you'll steer toward where the money is, not toward the truth.

XANTIPPE I know your intentions are good—Hades, as we know, is paved with good intentions—

SOCRATES   I'm happy to hear that it's paved at all. I'll probably spend a good deal of time there.

XANTIPPE   You will not charge money for lessons?

SOCRATES   No, I will not.

XANTIPPE   How are we to live?

SOCRATES   I'll sell those sandals Alcibiades gave me. The workmanship is fabulous.

XANTIPPE   And after that?

SOCRATES   Who knows?

XANTIPPE   It's not only the money, Socrates. It's that you're not liked. You're hated by many people. Hated because you refuse to fit in.

SOCRATES   Perhaps because they have no hold over me.

XANTIPPE   You see—I'm afraid for you. If you'd set up as a teacher and were paid you'd be one of them—they'd accept you. But as it is you're completely uncontrollable. You're known as the horsefly of Athens, and you sting the most respectable people on their least respectable parts. You can't expect to be popular.

SOCRATES   No, a horsefly is never popular among horses.

XANTIPPE   [*Turning away*] It's no use. I'm thinking of you and how to help you, and you think I'm thinking of myself.

SOCRATES   I was in love with you when we married, Xantippe. I'm an old codger now, but I'm still in love with you as much as an ancient party can be—

XANTIPPE   Yes, I know about that. You explained at one of those bachelor revels you attend that you wanted to achieve self-control—and a debater who could keep his temper in the same house with Xantippe was equal to anything. So you married me.

SOCRATES Who told you that?

XANTIPPE Oh, a lot of people came running to me with that.

SOCRATES A man says a lot of things to amuse the company, but I never said quite that.

XANTIPPE You've never loved me!

SOCRATES Xantippe, you come right after Athens—next to the city of Athens I love you best. . . .

XANTIPPE Yes, after the entire city of Athens—

SOCRATES No, after the beauty of the city of Athens, and after its art and wisdom and knowledge, I love you best and I've always loved you best.
[*He goes to her and puts his arms about her*]
I'm a horrible old satyr, and enough to frighten any woman, but if you can overlook that I'm as much yours as you're mine. It's not much of a life for you—

XANTIPPE Who cares about that and who cares about a man's looks? I'm no beauty. I was homely to begin with and I haven't improved. I was lucky to get you. I'd have been lucky to get anybody, but that doesn't mean I'm willing to share you with somebody else! I've never believed this story of yours that it's Athens you're in love with. There's a woman. I've smelled her perfume on you more than once.

SOCRATES Let's not be ridiculous! Perfume!

[*He moves away from her*]

XANTIPPE There are women at these feasts of reason you attend.

SOCRATES Flute-players and dancers and entertainers, yes, sometimes.

XANTIPPE One particular woman with one particular perfume!

SOCRATES   Years ago then, so long that I've forgotten it.

XANTIPPE   So it wasn't Athens, after all!

SOCRATES   If you're thinking of the thing that makes a man wake in the morning happy to be alive, happy there's a new day to live, yes, it was Athens. I wish I could tell you what I feel for this city, Xantippe! This Athens, a gathering of slaves and free men, of artists and unprincipled traitors, of staggering genius and sure-footed dolts, of soaring altars to the gods built with stolen money, of levelheaded madmen who speak like their own goddess of wisdom and then filch the gold fringe from that goddess's image, a pack of poets who are generals, and of generals who grow rich by selling their prisoners, of men who are paragons of virtue and evil, who have done everything a man should do, and also everything he should not! A hive of inspired and brainy and reckless idiots, who love the arts more than money, and fame more than the arts, and politics more than all three! How they have done it I don't know, and they don't, but they've built such a city here as the gods must have been thinking of when they first made men—a city drowned in sunlight and dancing and music and wisdom and deviltry, and crowned with the mystic marbles of the Parthenon!

XANTIPPE   There was a woman too.

SOCRATES   Very well, there was a woman, a long time ago—but Athens has been the great love of my life, and after Athens, you. This is a golden place and we have lived through a golden age.

XANTIPPE   I've lived mostly in the kitchen. In the age of iron pots. But I've looked out enough to know that no matter how much you love Athens it doesn't love you. It loves beauty and glamour and success and it resents you for going about asking embarrassing questions.

SOCRATES   I have many friends.

XANTIPPE   You have a following, but if you want Athens to like you you do everything wrong. I know you want to do everything right, and that's why you eat little and wear old clothes and take no money and try to get at the truth. But Athens still wants beauty and glamour and success—not an old man in bare feet pointing out that the human race doesn't know its ass from its elbow.

SOCRATES   But it does! That's one of the few things it does know!

LAMPROC.   [*Calling from outside*] Father! Father!
[*He runs in*]
Father, there's an indictment of you hung up in the government building!

SOCRATES   An indictment of me?

LAMPROC.   Yes, of you!

XANTIPPE   Oh, God!

[CRITO *and his son* CRITOBULUS *enter, followed by* PHAEDO. *Crito and Phaedo are of Socrates' generation. All the newcomers are well to do, a fact which is reflected only in the quality of their dress, for the costume is unvarying*]

LAMPROC.   Crito took it down.

XANTIPPE   Oh, God help us!

LAMPROC.   Mother, you forget! You should go to the women's quarters.

XANTIPPE   Oh, should I? In a house when there's only one woman and she mistress, wife, mother, and slave, I see little sense in women's quarters!

SOCRATES   There's sense in that, Lamprocles. And Xantippe knows Crito, Critobulus, and Phaedo as well as we do. Come in, all three. Xantippe must hear this.

CRITO   It must have been hung up early this morning. I happened to notice it on my way to the jury room. It's very short: "We three citizens of Athens, Meletos, Anytas, and Lycon, bring this charge against Socrates—that he is guilty of crime, first because he does not worship the gods of our city, but introduces new divinities of his own; second, because he corrupts the thinking of our young men. We make this charge and demand an immediate trial. The penalty due is death."

XANTIPPE I knew this would happen!

SOCRATES I didn't. It's better than I could have hoped for. They've delivered themselves into my hands. They are fools in an argument, all of them.

XANTIPPE But they'll have you killed!

SOCRATES Perhaps you should go into the women's quarters, Xantippe.

XANTIPPE [*To Lamprocles*] Give me the fish, then. Somebody must cook, whatever happens. Give me the fish.

LAMPROC. What fish?

XANTIPPE You were sent for a fish.

LAMPROC. I didn't go to the market. I met Crito.

XANTIPPE Then where's the obol?

LAMPROC. What is the matter with you, mother? Will you be quiet and go?

XANTIPPE You were given an obol to buy fish!

LAMPROC. [*Giving her the coin*] Here! Who wants an obol now?

XANTIPPE I do. We have only two, and they're probably our last. Proceed with your discussion, gentlemen. I take my smaller brain to another apartment.

[*She goes out*]

LAMPROC. What is the meaning of this? Why should they suddenly demand my father's death?

PHAEDO It's no sudden thing. It's been coming for a long time.

SOCRATES   It's a heaven-sent opportunity to defend my way of life in
            open court. And Athens will laugh them into exile. In any
            other city there'd be doubt of the outcome. Here, among the
            clear heads of the merry Greeks it's unalloyed good fortune.
            I'll win and they'll pay and never hear the end of it.

CRITO   And yet, if you could avoid this trial, I'd hope for that.

SOCRATES   I wouldn't. The lesser divinity that gets so exercised when
            I'm about to do something wrong has said not a word of
            protest. If he were concerned he'd have me out of town before
            nightfall. Not a peep from him. He's happy.
            [*A pretty woman of thirty-five or forty comes in slowly and
            gravely. Socrates sees her first*]
            Theodote! Why have you come here?

THEODOTE   Forgive me. Forgive me for the news I bring. I bring the
            most terrible news that could come to Athens.

CRITO   We know about the indictment.

THEODOTE   Forget the indictment. Forget all your lives up to this time.
            We have lost the war. Athens has been beaten at Aegospo-
            tami. We have lost our fleet. Our city, which has ruled so
            long, is at the mercy of Sparta. I come to tell this to the one
            great man left out of the great age of Athens. Pericles is dead,
            Herodotus is dead. Sophocles, too, and Euripides—and
            Alcibiades. I bring the message to Socrates.

            [XANTIPPE *re-enters and listens*]

SOCRATES   Where did you hear it?

THEODOTE   Three runners came from Piraeus. The Spartans won by
            sheer trickery—from us who have always won by trickery—
            who have outtricked the world. Four mornings in a row our
            fleet approached their harbor and offered battle. Each morn-
            ing their fleet refused combat. On the fourth morning, after
            our fleet had returned to its base and anchored and dismissed
            the men to baths and breakfast, the Spartan fleet appeared
            round the point, took our men and admirals off guard,

captured every ship, every man—butchered many, saved a few of the wealthy to be ransomed. King Pausanias of Sparta is at Piraeus now. He offers no terms, demands abject surrender.

LAMPROC. Never!

XANTIPPE What will you fight with? With that secondhand sword and shield you were planning to buy?

SOCRATES Has the Assembly been called?

THEODOTE It's meeting at midday, at the government building.

SOCRATES It's near midday now. We'll all be needed there. Come, gentlemen.

[*The men go out, leaving the two women.* THEODOTE *starts to go*]

XANTIPPE Then there's to be no trial?

THEODOTE There's no time for such things now.

XANTIPPE Thank God for that much. Who are you?

THEODOTE Theodote. You are Xantippe?

XANTIPPE I am.

THEODOTE I'd better go.

XANTIPPE My reputation frightens you, no doubt.

THEODOTE I've heard of your talent for invective.

XANTIPPE From whom?

THEODOTE That's a professional secret.

XANTIPPE Yes, of course. You're a strumpet.

THEODOTE Oh, why put it so mildly? An alien whore from Ionia, a foreign bitch with all the advantages and accomplishments denied the native born.

XANTIPPE An excellent debater's trick. Always describe your vices as virtues. You learned that from Socrates?

THEODOTE Anybody who has studied under a Sophist has learned that trick.

XANTIPPE You have studied under Sophists?

THEODOTE I was never sure whether I was learning or teaching.

XANTIPPE If you were doing what I think, you were teaching, dear child, you were teaching. May I look at the hem of your himation?

THEODOTE [*Backing away*] There's nothing unusual about it.

XANTIPPE Stand still, Ionian, I won't hurt you.
[*She smells the garment*]
Yes, it was your perfume he brought home.

THEODOTE That water-drinking old Silenus of yours? Never! I deny it!

XANTIPPE I wanted to know, and now I know.

[PHOENIX *comes in*]

PHOENIX Mother, there are many soldiers in the street, and they march and won't look at me!

THEODOTE The Spartans!

XANTIPPE Yes, go to your work and double your prices. Find yourself an officer. Take him to bed.

THEODOTE Keep to your kitchen, wife. Save what food you have.

[*She goes*]

PHOENIX I want to see the soldiers.

XANTIPPE No, stay with me. It's not safe outside.

[*They go out*]

END OF SCENE

Act One

SCENE: *Several months later. Socrates, Phaedo, Crito, Anytas, Lycon Crassos, Meletos, and Critobulus are working with crowbars to overturn a section (or fragment) of the city wall.*

SOCRATES   Another bar or two under this side, friends, and we'll have it down to the required level.

CRITO   I can never get used to tearing down the walls of my own city.

SOCRATES   It's better not to get used to that.

PHAEDO   But we promised to tear down our walls—and the Spartans will be on our necks here till it's done. We'd better appear to be working. Satyros is approaching.

[SATYROS, *a gigantic thug carrying a whip and followed by two other thugs, likewise armed, comes in and watches for a moment*]

SATYROS   Turn this way!
[*The workers turn to face Satyros*]
There has been loitering here! I saw it! Let me remind you of the decree! The treaty between Sparta and Athens provides that the walls of Athens be razed to the ground by her own citizens! The work is nearly done, but now a few fools say they will do no more! Critias and King Pausanias are inspecting the work at this moment, and no excuses will be accepted! Those who loiter will be whipped! Those who refuse—will be killed! Put your weight behind those tools!
[*The group resumes its work.* CRITIAS *and* KING PAUSANIAS *enter. Critias is an elegant and intelligent Athenian; Pausanias is unpolished, slow moving, hesitant in speech. The workers make a good deal of noise with their tools*]
Don't disturb the king and the general, you there! Take yourselves a bit further off!

[SOCRATES *and the men with him move off stage, but can still be heard chunking and prying.* SATYROS *follows them*]

CRITIAS   The work has gone slowly, King Pausanias, but, as you can see, it's nearly finished.

PAUSANIAS Lord love you, don't call me King Pausanias. The name's long enough without the handle.

CRITIAS   I shall feel insolent if I give you no title, O King—

PAUSANIAS Your name's Critias, isn't it? You're the brilliant Critias.

CRITIAS   I am Critias, yes.

PAUSANIAS All right, I'll call you Brilliant and you call me Stupid, the way they do in Sparta—

CRITIAS   Stupid—?

PAUSANIAS Bless you, yes—Stupid. In Sparta all the kings are called Stupid, and they are stupid. That's really the only qualification of the royal house down there. My family has an almost perfect record, nobody closer than a second cousin has learned to read during the last three centuries.

CRITIAS   But you read, of course?

PAUSANIAS Read? I can't write my name! A monarch who could read would be booted out of Laconia. And rightly, too. Stupid I was born, stupid I live, stupid I shall die, and the better king for it!

CRITIAS   I suspect that you are . . . not quite . . . forthright—

PAUSANIAS No, no! I tell the simple stupid truth about everything. That's the advantage of having a fool for a king. A fool can afford to be sincere. Everybody trusts him. So trust me, come on. Be my friend, call me Stupid.

CRITIAS   I can't.

PAUSANIAS Satyros, come here!
           [SATYROS re-enters]
           I order you to call me Stupid.

CRITIAS   [*In an agony of indecision*] Yes—Stupid.

PAUSANIAS Good. Now we can be friends, Brilliant. That's all, Satyros.
          [SATYROS *goes out*]
          You were about to tell me something when I interrupted
          you.

CRITIAS   I was about to make a report.

PAUSANIAS Put it in words of one syllable, please.

CRITIAS   Surely. It was easy to destroy democracy here in Athens,
           but it's not so easy to make the Athenians like the oligarchy
           which we have set up in its place. As the head of the thirty
           oligarchs I am extremely unpopular.

PAUSANIAS How do you know?

CRITIAS   Remarks are made about me, even to my face, which leave
           no doubt.

PAUSANIAS You could strangle those who make remarks, Brilliant.

CRITIAS   Yes, we could, St— O King—but my method has been to
           entrust them with authority.

PAUSANIAS The leaders who oppose you—you give them authority?

CRITIAS   Yes.

PAUSANIAS Why don't they continue to oppose you when in office?

CRITIAS   Well, they don't. They're on our side, you see. They've taken
           money from our treasury. They're involved in what we're
           doing.

PAUSANIAS I see.

CRITIAS   After that their hands aren't any too clean. They're working
           with us. That shuts them up.

PAUSANIAS Blackmail.

CRITIAS   That's not the word we use.

PAUSANIAS It's a word I know. Two syllables, but familiar.

CRITIAS   Well, we find these men, talk to them, and bring them over to
           our side. At the moment the most outspoken and venomous
           of our opponents is this man Socrates whom you saw working
           here just now—

PAUSANIAS Socrates?

CRITIAS   You know the name?

PAUSANIAS Everybody knows about him. He's the one that goes barefoot
           and talks but never writes anything down. I should like to see
           him.

CRITIAS   He's in that labor gang.

PAUSANIAS I should like to hear him talk, too.

CRITIAS   Nothing easier to arrange.
           [*He calls*]
           Satyros! [*To the king*] He'll talk you blind.
           [SATYROS *enters*]
           Bring that group here.

           [SATYROS *goes out, can be heard calling*]

SATYROS   This way, dogs! This way, Athenians! Bring your tools.

           [SOCRATES *and the others enter*]

CRITIAS   The king of Sparta has expressed a wish to hear Socrates
           talk. What do you wish to hear him say, O King?

           [SATYROS *re-enters*]

PAUSANIAS I want to hear him talk the way he talks. One of those ques-
           tion and answer things people are always telling about.

CRITIAS   You hear, Socrates?

SOCRATES   With whom shall I speak, my dear Critias?

CRITIAS   With anybody.

SOCRATES   Very well. King Pausanias—

PAUSANIAS   No, no, I don't want to be tied up in knots! Choose a social equal.

SOCRATES   Surely. Anytas, we began a conversation a moment ago—

CRITIAS   Good. Complete it—for the king.

SOCRATES   I believe the last thing you said was that you were my enemy?

ANYTAS   It was! You've spent your whole life pulling Athens down, stone by stone, and this is a fitting climax to your work! The defeat of Athens, the thousands dead of famine and pestilence, the pestilential government that rules us now under Sparta's orders, these are all the result of Socrates' teachings!

SOCRATES   Please answer my question, Anytas, and do not make orations. Are you my enemy?

ANYTAS   I am!

SOCRATES   Anytas, is a man's enemy one who does evil to him?

ANYTAS   He is.

SOCRATES   And is a man's friend one who does good to him?

ANYTAS   He is.

SOCRATES   Now, Anytas, my friends tell me that I am a wise teacher and a philosopher of parts. Is that true?

ANYTAS   It is not. It's a lie.

SOCRATES   Then my friends flatter me and lie to me?

ANYTAS   They do.

SOCRATES Is that good for me?
          [*Anytas hesitates*]
          Is that good for me?

ANYTAS   No.

SOCRATES My enemies, on the other hand, tell me bluntly to my face
          that I am a fool and a windbag. Is that good for me?

ANYTAS   It's the truth!

SOCRATES But is it good for me?

ANYTAS   How do I know?

SOCRATES Are you afraid to answer?

PAUSANIAS By God, if he answers he'll contradict himself!

CRITIAS   That's true. That's what always happens.

SOCRATES Is it good for me to be told that I am a fool and windbag?

ANYTAS   Yes, damn you, yes! Because you are!

SOCRATES But you began by saying that a friend was one who did good
          to a man and an enemy was one who did evil—and you end
          by saying that the friend does evil to him and the enemy does
          good.

PAUSANIAS Wonderful! Now that I understand! Philosophy without one
          two-syllable word!

CRITIAS   Do not be misled by him, O King; he is your mortal enemy
          and mine, and no matter how much his tricks may amuse us
          the state we have set up here will not be safe while men like
          him go about questioning the wisdom of the gods and the
          accuracy of common definitions.

SOCRATES Perhaps you shouldn't blame me if your state is unsafe,
          Critias. No state is safe, no definition is quite accurate.

CRITIAS   Don't hide behind that! You attack us daily. You attack the present government and defend democracy!

SOCRATES   Of course I do, Critias. I like to walk up and down the streets questioning and doubting.

PAUSANIAS I'd like to ask this man a stupid question.

CRITIAS   You'll get a stupid answer, but ask it.

PAUSANIAS When Athens and Sparta were enemies did Athens do good to Sparta?

SOCRATES   Much good, O King.

PAUSANIAS Will you make that clear to me?

SOCRATES   Is a victory good or evil?

PAUSANIAS Good.

SOCRATES   Is a victory possible without an enemy?

PAUSANIAS No.

SOCRATES   Was not the victory of Sparta made possible by her enemy Athens?

PAUSANIAS Yes, by the loins of Helen, yes! And did Sparta do good to Athens?

SOCRATES   Yes. When you took our freedom from us, then for the first time we realized what a precious thing freedom is!

LYCON   Oh, stay with him! Go right on asking him questions! He'll teach you that up is down and east is west and left is right and young is old and a father is no wiser than his son and the gods are fictional characters invented by Homer and—

CRASSOS   He will not! He'll ask you if you're sure that left is always left and right is always right, and then he'll show you that it depends on the point of view, and then he'll point out that because a man's in authority doesn't always mean he's right, and even parents know less about their children's diseases than a doctor knows and—!

LYCON   And what a string of rubbish that is!

SOCRATES   There's truth in what your father says, Crassos. Too much zeal has made you incoherent. And yet every point you tried to make could have been made, and convincingly, if you had taken your time and found the right words.

CRASSOS   I'm sorry . . .

SOCRATES   But nobody is born with poise. Even kings have to learn that.

PAUSANIAS   Is this what you call democracy?

CRITIAS   This is democracy. Have you had enough of it? May I change the subject now?

PAUSANIAS   Yes. But democracy is as stupid as I am.

SOCRATES   As stupid as all of us put together, O King. But free!

CRITIAS   [To Satyros] Take them out. All but this man.
            [He points to Socrates. SATYROS and his thugs march the labor gang out, leaving Socrates, Critias, and Pausanias]
            You were my first teacher, Socrates. You are still my master, even though I am by accident master of Athens for this moment. I learned everything I know about the art of government from you. We have differed lately over methods and over what's expedient, but we both want the same thing: the best government that can be had for our great and beloved city.

SOCRATES   What do you want of me, Critias?

CRITIAS   Nothing, Socrates. Only your good will.

SOCRATES   If you wanted nothing you would not spray me with this expert nonsense.

            [XANTIPPE enters, carrying a stone jug and food wrapped in what looks like a cabbage leaf]

CRITIAS   What is your errand?

XANTIPPE   I'm bringing food for Socrates.

CRITIAS   Leave it. Or come back later.

SOCRATES   My dear Critias, Xantippe is not a woman one lightly sends
           away.

XANTIPPE   I'll come back.

           [*She goes out the way she came*]

CRITIAS   You are aware, Socrates, as well as I, that a man who governs
           a nation sits in a lonely place with great decisions in his hands,
           knowing that he is not worthy to make them and yet that they
           must be made—

SOCRATES   What do you want of me, Critias?

CRITIAS   Now unfortunately the government which we have here at
           present is not the democracy you love, yet it is the govern-
           ment of Athens, and if Athens is to endure through these
           dark days of defeat her government must be made effective.

           [PAUSANIAS *yawns—rises to look out*]

SOCRATES   What do you want me to do, Critias?

CRITIAS   Very well. There is, on the island of Salamis, a rich and un-
           scrupulous man named Leon who openly defies Athens and
           has sworn that he will contribute nothing to the treasury
           while the Thirty are in power. The Thirty wishes you to sit in
           judgment at his trial.

SOCRATES   I am willing to act as a judge. He has been indicted under the
           laws?

CRITIAS   His crimes are so open and flagrant that there seems no need
           for formal indictment.

           [XANTIPPE *returns and listens, unseen by Critias or Socrates*]

SOCRATES   But how can a judge act if there is no indictment?

CRITIAS   You have said that you will act.

SOCRATES   As a judge, according to the laws.

CRITIAS   We have been obliged to abrogate the usual laws and set up special panels for trying these cases. You would sit as a member of such a panel.

SOCRATES   There would be other judges on this case?

CRITIAS   There will be five altogether.

SOCRATES   I should be one among five. My voice would hardly count.

CRITIAS   Your presence would count for a great deal.

SOCRATES   It is likely that Leon would be found guilty?

CRITIAS   It is very likely.

SOCRATES   Not certain?

CRITIAS   Perhaps certain.

SOCRATES   And what is the probable penalty?

CRITIAS   Death, I should think, for such a crime.

SOCRATES   What is his crime?

CRITIAS   Disobedience.

SOCRATES   Disobedience to the Thirty?

CRITIAS   Yes.

[SOCRATES *turns his head as if listening*]

SOCRATES   No, Critias, I shall not sit on such a court.

CRITIAS   Before you say no finally, Socrates, let me warn you that I am
           not alone in the government, and that I am not always able to
           control it. If you sit with this court you will be part of the
           government and fairly safe. If you do not accept the position
           on the panel it may be that you yourself will be brought be-
           fore just such a judge as I ask you to become. Why are you
           silent?

SOCRATES   I am listening.

CRITIAS   To whom?

SOCRATES   There is a little fellow, invisible and nameless, who sits on my
           ear at such moments and whispers to me. He is saying some-
           thing now.

CRITIAS   Listen, then. I shall give you—while that eagle crosses the sky.

           [THEODOTE *enters opposite Xantippe. She carries an elegant
           flask, a basket of food, and a bunch of grapes*]

PAUSANIAS [*Who has wandered to that side of the stage*] What is your errand
           here, sweetheart?

THEODOTE   I'm bringing food for Anytas, darling.

PAUSANIAS That reminds me, I'm famishing.

THEODOTE   This is not for you.

PAUSANIAS Do you think Anytas would mind?

THEODOTE   He paid for it, lover.

PAUSANIAS But I'm devilish hungry!

THEODOTE   Does that make a difference?

PAUSANIAS It had better. Sit down, dearest. Let's see what we have here.

THEODOTE   Let it alone!

PAUSANIAS [*Taking her by the arm*] Be more courteous to outlanders.

THEODOTE [*Striking him with her free hand*] It's not for Spartans.

PAUSANIAS [*Forcing her to sit*] A little service, please.

[*He takes the food*]

THEODOTE You're horrible.

PAUSANIAS I know.
[*He sits*]
Stupid, too, don't you think?

THEODOTE Yes, stupid.

PAUSANIAS That's what they all say. But I am the king of Sparta.

THEODOTE The king of Sparta! And I said you were stupid! Oh, forgive me!

[XANTIPPE *crouches, listening*]

SOCRATES The three most gifted young men I have ever known sat talking with me through the whole of a summer night, about twenty-five years ago. Their names were Alcibiades, Charmides, and Critias, for you were one of the three. We talked of Athens and of the arts and of government . . . and of the chances of this world. And we concluded—I think it was you, Critias, who summed up for us, and we were happy in what you said—we concluded that the most valuable thing a man or a state could have was freedom. We concluded that if a man or a state was to retain freedom three things were needed: power and incorruptibility and frugality—the art of wanting little for yourself. And the more frugal and honest you are the less power you need.

CRITIAS Must we go back so far?

SOCRATES I had great hope for you three, and for Athens because of you. A democracy must have leaders and perhaps another Pericles might come from among you. You were very gay, and witty and elated, and somebody proposed that we swear an oath to support democracy whatever might come. We made up such an oath, and swore it, all four of us. The oath was to this effect: "I will kill with my own hand, if I am able, any man who subverts the democracy of Athens, or who shall hold any office in the city after the democracy has been destroyed, or shall rise in arms to make himself a despot, or shall help a despot to establish himself. And if anyone else slay such an enemy of our democracy I will account the slayer holy before the gods and give him friendship and love." Do you remember this?

CRITIAS   I remember. Men do silly things when a little drunk.

SOCRATES   And when drunk with power—or the thirst for power. That was twenty-five years ago. Charmides is dead. He was among the first to plot the destruction of democracy, and he is dead. Alcibiades—you know his history. He set out to gain power at any price. He poured out money. He offered the most extravagant displays of games and horse racing and costly celebration in our city's history. He took money, in vast quantity, from the king of Persia, promising Athens to him. He was banished, and set out to destroy the city that banished him. He was a brilliant statesman and general, and he betrayed every talent and every trust till he was universally hated—and at last his enemies caught up with him and he was killed. The history of Athens reeks with such men, brilliant and unscrupulous, committed to success at any price, serving on three sides of every cause—and they have not ended well. Themistocles, our greatest general, saved Athens from Persia, and then sold out to Persia—and died dishonored. In all our history there has never been a time when brilliant men have been lacking to betray our city and change coats for money— and die young. You are still young, Critias, and you, like the others, have sold out—and you follow after Alcibiades.

CRITIAS   You lie. I have not sold out.

SOCRATES   Leon is guilty of no crime. You wish to kill him to consolidate your power and to confiscate his fortune. You have killed many because they were rich and fat and tempting prizes. You will die young.

CRITIAS   It is too late for you to die young, Socrates.

SOCRATES   Much too late. And I have no fortune.

CRITIAS   Satyros has plans for you. I have seen him look at your throat.

SOCRATES   The gods have plans for all of us.

CRITIAS   Satyros could be placated.

SOCRATES   But not the gods.

CRITIAS   You believe in the gods?

SOCRATES   Yes, in all of them. And especially in the one that tells me not to sit on your court.

[CRITIAS *takes a step toward Socrates to deliver some sort of ultimatum but is interrupted by the entrance of the rest of the labor gang.* PHAEDO, CRITO, *and* CRASSOS *come in with food in their hands;* ANYTAS *sees Theodote and goes to her, expecting to receive his collation from her.* SATYROS *enters with his thugs*]

ANYTAS   You brought food for me?

THEODOTE   Yes, I did, Anytas, but our friend, the king of Sparta, was very hungry, and I knew you'd want him to have it.

PAUSANIAS I'm sorry, friend, but I was ravenous and a pretty girl came along with some good-looking fruits and vegetables—
[*He goes on eating*]
and I haven't got the heart to give them back.

ANYTAS   You intend to finish the lot?

PAUSANIAS I do.

ANYTAS   [*To Theodote*] Here's a drachma; bring me something.

[THEODOTE *rises*]

PAUSANIAS I'm sorry, friend. She stays with me.

ANYTAS   I'll get something for myself.

          [*He starts out.* THEODOTE *sits again*]

SATYROS   Be back before the sun crosses the wall.

          [ANYTAS *goes out without speaking. The newcomers settle them-
          selves to eat*]

CRITIAS   Before the sun touches the west pillars of the Acropolis you
          will be at the Senate chamber, ready to join the other four
          judges.

SOCRATES In the old days the city of Athens seemed to us an imperfect
          place, riddled with treachery and rivalry, and yet, compared
          with any other city a city of light—because it allowed men's
          minds to be free. It is now a despotism, and you govern it,
          but you have it in your power to give us back our city of light.
          Remember the days of your youth, Critias, and give it back.
          Forget these murders that make you rich and this corruption
          of free men that keeps you in power—

CRITIAS   [*Flashing out*] Whatever I believe you taught me! What I do
          you taught me to do!

SOCRATES Indeed?

CRITIAS   Did you not teach us to question our gods, our laws, our
          customs, and the very meaning of the words we used?

SOCRATES It was our way to question everything.

CRITIAS   And did we find anything sure?

SOCRATES Nothing sure, worse luck.

CRITIAS   Then why not murder, why not rob, why not take what you
          want where you find it? There are no rules!

SOCRATES [*Quietly*] But while we are at it, Critias, should we not also question the value of murder, the value of blood money, the value of high office in the state illegally attained, before we destroy all we have to possess them?

CRITIAS   [*To Satyros*] Stay with him. If he goes to the Senate do not touch him. If he goes to his home, or elsewhere, follow him and do the needful.

SATYROS   Yes, master.

[CRITIAS *goes out*]

SOCRATES [*To Satyros*] Why, it seems that we are to be well acquainted; you are to be my constant companion.

SATYROS   To the death, Socrates!

SOCRATES You hear that? He has a sense of humor!

[XANTIPPE *goes to Socrates*]

XANTIPPE What are you going to do?

SOCRATES I believe you have something to eat there in your hand. I shall begin with that.

[*She gives him the packet and the jug*]

XANTIPPE You could eat on the way. You must be at the Senate chamber before the sun reaches the west wall.

SOCRATES I'm thinking of writing a hymn to Apollo. I'm growing so appallingly old, forgive the pun, and I love the sun so much, and a man should write down a little something before he dies, even if it's bad.

XANTIPPE You can write a hymn while you sit on his court.

SOCRATES I'm not going to the Senate. I shall go home.

SATYROS   I knew it would come! I knew it!

XANTIPPE But this monster is waiting here to kill you!

SOCRATES Let him wait. A man must have his lunch.

> [*He eats*]

PAUSANIAS Better do as you're told, friend.

THEODOTE Yes, you must!

XANTIPPE Give me that food! Go! Go! To the Senate!

> [*She takes the food*]

SOCRATES All my life I've been saying it is better for a man to die than to do what his soul believes to be wrong. Shall I now do wrong to save my life?

PAUSANIAS He will have Leon killed anyway.

XANTIPPE With you or without you he will do this murder! You can't stop him. Why must you die too?

SOCRATES Please give me my food, Xantippe. I've been working since dawn.

> [XANTIPPE *gives him the food again, and sits with bowed head*]

END OF SCENE

Act One

SCENE: *Socrates' house about half an hour later. Lysis and Phoenix are seated at the table, the bread and the jug before them.*

PHOENIX   Why can't I have any more?

LYSIS   Because that's what she said to give you; just that much and not another crust.

PHOENIX   Where is she?

LYSIS   She went to take food to father. There's somebody coming now.

[*The children get up and slip into a corner.* SOCRATES *comes in with* XANTIPPE *and followed by* SATYROS *and his thugs.* PHOENIX *runs to Xantippe*]

XANTIPPE   Are you all right?

PHOENIX   Lysis won't give me any more.

XANTIPPE   I told him how much to give you. The rest's for supper.

[SATYROS *looks at the family scene and moves to a place where he can wait*]

SOCRATES   You know, that was a long walk in the sun. I'd be happy to moisten my throat with a little wine and water—if the needful is to be postponed at all.

SATYROS   Have your drink. Pausanias wishes to watch this affair.

SOCRATES   Maybe you'll have a sup with me then?

SATYROS   You wouldn't drink with me. I'm a slave. And an executioner.

SOCRATES   You have scruples about drinking with me?

35

SATYROS   No citizen drinks with a slave.

SOCRATES   Nonsense. Pour for both of us, Xantippe. And for yourself.
           [XANTIPPE *does so*]
           Sit down.

SATYROS   It's not right.

SOCRATES   You'll get used to it.

SATYROS   Pausanias will find me at the table.

SOCRATES   He has no principles. Sit.

SATYROS   I'll drink standing.

SOCRATES   You're frightened. Well, you make many enemies. Perhaps
           you should be wary.

           [XANTIPPE *serves Socrates first, then Satyros*]

SATYROS   I've never before drunk wine with a free citizen.

SOCRATES   How does it taste?

SATYROS   Excellent.

XANTIPPE   Where's Lamprocles?

LYSIS   He's got a sword and a shield and he went to Piraeus.

XANTIPPE   Piraeus.

LYSIS   You see, there's a rebellion starting against Critias at Piraeus.
           Meletos is leading it. Critobulus went—and Anytas, too.

SOCRATES   Anytas? We just saw him.

LYSIS   Well, he went with the rebels. And he was mad. And a lot of
           them went. They were singing and swishing around with their
           swords and making a lot of noise.

SOCRATES   I should be there.

XANTIPPE   You! At your age!

SOCRATES   At any age. And so we're to be honored by a visit from King
            Pausanias?

SATYROS   I don't know whether it's an honor, but he's coming here. He
            wants to see how a philosopher takes it.

XANTIPPE   Socrates!

SOCRATES   Yes.

XANTIPPE   Kiss the children and I'll take them away.

SOCRATES   Let's not worry the children, Xantippe. They'll have troubles
            soon enough.

XANTIPPE   But—look at them!

            [*She points to Satyros and his men*]

SOCRATES   Yes, they look frightening, but . . . it's perhaps an illusion.
            [CRITIAS *and* PAUSANIAS *enter*]
            Ah, the whole power of the state is with us!
            [THEODOTE *enters*]
            And it becomes a social occasion! Sit, gentlemen, if you can
            find places. We're not equipped for much company.

PAUSANIAS   If I may make a suggestion?

SOCRATES   Yes?

PAUSANIAS   There is such a place as the women's quarters, I'm told, in
            Athenian houses.

SOCRATES   Yes, there is.

PAUSANIAS   If the women and children would enter those quarters—

THEODOTE   Oh, not I! I'm not supposed to enter the women's apartment.
            I'm only supposed to mix with men!

PAUSANIAS Stay here, then, but let the wife and children retire.

[XANTIPPE *looks at Socrates, who smiles back calmly, then she grimly takes the children and goes*]

CRITIAS I have many things to do, you know! It's unnecessary and irregular that I should be here.

[THEODOTE *sits quietly in a corner*]

PAUSANIAS You will remain till it's over, my dear Critias.

CRITIAS Then get it over!

PAUSANIAS Certainly. But there was a question I wished to ask this Socrates. You will answer?

SOCRATES As well as I can.

PAUSANIAS You said something about some small divinity that clings to your ear and gives you advice. . . .

SOCRATES Yes.

PAUSANIAS Now, this is very interesting to me, because I've got something like that, too.

SOCRATES You have? Well that's very interesting to me.

PAUSANIAS It's like this. You have the kind of brain that cuts corners and goes in and out of ratholes like nothing. You're quick and you can figure things out—only every once in a while this little demon of yours leans over and says to you, "Wait a minute. Not so fast."

SOCRATES He says something like that, yes.

PAUSANIAS Now I'm just the opposite. I'm dull. You go in and out of that rathole in front of my eyes and I can't even see where you went. I can't figure anything out. So what happens? I'm a king and I have to make decisions because people come screaming at me. And what do I do? I wait.

SOCRATES   And somebody whispers in your ear?

PAUSANIAS No. Nobody whispers in my ear. No such luck. I just wait and let them scream. And if I wait long enough, and sleep on it, and maybe sleep on it two or three times, why I wake up some morning and there it is, plain as morning, what to do.

SOCRATES   Why, that's wonderful!

PAUSANIAS And I'm stupid! Dumb!

SOCRATES   Just beyond words wonderful!

PAUSANIAS Isn't it?

CRITIAS   Could we abbreviate these felicitations?

PAUSANIAS Isn't it wonderful?

SOCRATES   Beyond description! Enchanting!

PAUSANIAS Now take a case like this: Critias says Socrates is the worst enemy of the state and we must be rid of him at once. At once, mind you. Now that's what I don't like. Maybe we should get rid of you, but why all this hurry? Why not sleep on it?

SOCRATES   Surely. Why not?

PAUSANIAS If need be, why not sleep—well . . . two or three nights on it?

SOCRATES   Of course I'm not a young man. If you wait too long I might die.

PAUSANIAS Now you're going round corners. Now you're too fast for me.

SOCRATES   I wonder.

PAUSANIAS Tell me, what is your little angel-demon whispering to you this afternoon?

SOCRATES Let me see. Something very strange. For the first time since I have known him he's whispering a warning about somebody else—not about me at all.

PAUSANIAS A warning?

SOCRATES Just a warning that somebody is in danger.

PAUSANIAS Not you?

SOCRATES Not me.

PAUSANIAS Me?

SOCRATES Not you.

PAUSANIAS [*Looking round*] Theodote?

SOCRATES No.

PAUSANIAS Your wife? Your children?

SOCRATES No.

PAUSANIAS Leon of Salamis?

SOCRATES No.

PAUSANIAS I can tell you something about Leon of Salamis. He's dead. Critias had him killed before he asked you to act as judge over him.

SOCRATES Is this true, Critias?

CRITIAS I am not here to be questioned.

PAUSANIAS It's true.

SOCRATES This is most strange and disturbing. Critias, the warning I receive concerns you, and it's so definite and immediate that I feel like urging you to run—run until you can surround yourself with heavy-armed troops and ward off what seems to be coming. . . .

CRITIAS   Thank you, I shall not run, and I am not especially enter-
tained. We are here, or at least I came here, for a certain pur-
pose, and my time is limited. You may have time to waste.
Philosophers and kings are taken care of by other people, but
every moment of my day is carefully planned, and this visit
was not even listed. The king wished me to be present and I
am present, but the business must be dispatched or I must
leave.

SOCRATES   I am more and more puzzled by this, Critias, but truly you
appear to be in danger here, and should leave quickly.

CRITIAS   You have talked yourself out of many tight corners, Socrates,
but you will not slip out of this one. Come.

PAUSANIAS   I'd prefer a little more time—

CRITIAS   I know. You'd prefer to wait till he dies of old age, as he sug-
gests. But patient though I am I'm not that patient. Come.

[*He stands at the door, inviting them out*]

PAUSANIAS   You are ready?

SOCRATES   As ready as I'm likely to be.

PAUSANIAS   Let's go then.

SOCRATES   Shall I precede you?

PAUSANIAS   If you will.

[SOCRATES, PAUSANIAS, *and then* CRITIAS *go out.* SATYROS *and
his men follow as usual.* THEODOTE *rises and runs to the door,
looking after them, then walks about the room; finally gets up
courage to go to the inner door*]

THEODOTE   Xantippe! Xantippe!

XANTIPPE [*At the doorway*] What is it?

THEODOTE May I come in with you?

XANTIPPE Why?

THEODOTE They've all gone out together. I don't want to be alone.

XANTIPPE Where have they gone?

THEODOTE I don't know.
[XANTIPPE *goes to the outside door, looks out, then comes back*]
What are they doing?

XANTIPPE They're walking away—the three of them—and Satyros is following with the executioners.

THEODOTE May I come in with you?

XANTIPPE Yes, come in.

[*She puts her arm around Theodote and the two women go together into the women's quarters, Theodote sobbing. The stage is empty and silent for a moment, then a man's cry is heard, quickly smothered.* XANTIPPE *returns, followed by* THEODOTE. *They stand near the inner door, looking at the outer one but not approaching it*]

THEODOTE What can we do now?

XANTIPPE Nothing. There's never anything a woman can do.

THEODOTE Will they bring him back?

XANTIPPE I don't know. There's nothing a woman can do. You or I or any of us now. . . . I don't care what he did. There was nobody like him. I don't care if he did have his arms round you. He could do as he pleased, no matter what I said. There was nobody like him.

THEODOTE Nobody.

XANTIPPE   He's probably lying in the open street. They leave them that way sometimes, the brutes. Will you help me carry him in?

THEODOTE   Yes, Xantippe. You were his wife. He loved you.

XANTIPPE   I don't know who he loved, but let's carry him in.
[THEODOTE *throws her arms round Xantippe, who remains stolid*]
Come, Theodote; we can cry afterward.

THEODOTE   [*Still crying*] I'm such a fool!

XANTIPPE   Well, who isn't? We're all fools.

THEODOTE   He . . . he wasn't.

XANTIPPE   I thought not at first. But he was. You weren't married to him.

THEODOTE   No. You'd know.

[*She controls herself*]

XANTIPPE   Can we go now?

THEODOTE   Yes.

[*They turn toward the outer door, their minds made up. At this moment* PAUSANIAS *comes in slowly and the women pause, looking at him.* SOCRATES *enters, looking back out the door. Xantippe sees him with incredulous relief*]

XANTIPPE   You! Socrates! What has happened?

SOCRATES   [*Bewildered*] I don't know, my dear. The usual governmental inefficiency. They killed the wrong man.

XANTIPPE   They killed—what man?

SOCRATES   Critias. They killed Critias.

XANTIPPE   Critias dead? And you're—not in danger?

SOCRATES   No, Stupid here is my friend—so far, anyway.

XANTIPPE   We were about to go out and carry you in, I and this scented
           doxy of yours!
           [*She moves violently away from Theodote*]
           That won't be necessary now!

SOCRATES   No, I can walk. You don't seem glad to see me.

XANTIPPE   I'm just so used to tricks I don't know what to think.

SOCRATES   Well, this was no trick. . . . I'm somewhat shaken. Critias
           did not make a handsome corpse. He didn't expect to die—
           and didn't intend to. He . . . struggled.

PAUSANIAS May I sit down?

SOCRATES   Oh, forgive me! Please sit down. King Pausanias of Sparta;
           my wife, Xantippe. You know Theodote.

XANTIPPE   He knows me too, I think. But if he knows any good of me
           that's more than I can say for him.

PAUSANIAS Thank you, lady. I'll sit here. The truth is I had no intention
           of having him killed today but he forced my hand.

SOCRATES   His death was not a mistake?

PAUSANIAS No, no, quite regular. A little hurried. In fact he was pretty
           green for plucking, and could have gathered in several large
           and luscious plutocrats in the next few days.

THEODOTE   You did this to . . . to save . . . the plutocrats?

PAUSANIAS No. No, sweetheart.

SOCRATES   "Green for plucking," you said.

PAUSANIAS Yes. Not ripe. Not fully ripe. Not half as rich as he would
           have been a week from now.

SOCRATES   You intend to—profit by this assassination?

PAUSANIAS The kings of Sparta have sunk pretty low. The ephors are everything now. My family needs a fortune, preferably in gold. The old Spartan iron money is falling into disuse and gold begins to circulate down there. I was counting on Critias to re-establish the family fortunes. He'll still bring me quite a chunk. Leon of Salamis alone was worth near half a million.

SOCRATES Which you will receive?

PAUSANIAS Who else?

SOCRATES The families of the deceased men, I should think.

PAUSANIAS Critias' family?

SOCRATES No, the families of the men Critias killed and robbed.

PAUSANIAS I shall never understand democracy. Critias stole the money. I stole it from Critias and have it. Shall I try to give it back to the men Critias stole it from? How do I know who they stole it from? Or who *they* stole from? It's an endless chain. Much simpler to keep it.

SOCRATES Do you think that all money is stolen?

PAUSANIAS How else would anybody get it? But before we go into that let me explain that the occupation is over and I am leaving Athens. Naturally I had to dispose of Critias before I went.

SOCRATES Ah—you take the troops with you!

PAUSANIAS I do. The occupation is over.

SOCRATES Now, we shall miss you, but this is not entirely bad news, you realize. We had been wondering if Sparta intended to police us indefinitely.

PAUSANIAS My career is in Sparta, after all, and things are not going well for me down there in my absence. I have to get back quickly and begin to patch the holes in my political socks. The money will help a lot. I'll put somebody in my place here and pull out. Do you have any suggestions?

SOCRATES I do. Give us back our democracy.

PAUSANIAS Your democracy? Well, hardly! Choose a man who can be trusted and I'll set him up in power before I leave.

SOCRATES No man can be trusted.

PAUSANIAS Well, you have to trust somebody!

SOCRATES Nobody can be trusted with power.

PAUSANIAS What do you trust?

SOCRATES The citizens—the voters.

PAUSANIAS Look—democracy is an ugly and disorderly form of government. The people of a democracy have no respect for their superiors; they do what they please and say what they like and they actually charge a profit for supplying each other with the necessities of life!

SOCRATES Do you know a better kind of government?

PAUSANIAS The one we have in Sparta.

SOCRATES I've never traveled. What is it like?

PAUSANIAS Ah, there all men get the same wages and eat the same rations and—well, it's like a great army, every man in it working for the common good.

SOCRATES That sounds perfect!

PAUSANIAS It is perfect. All property is in common, you see, and no man attempts to get ahead of the others, because he can't—and there's no unseemly scramble for wealth and honors such as you have here.

SOCRATES Then you've invented paradise.

PAUSANIAS I think we have.

SOCRATES Who governs this paradise?

PAUSANIAS The ephors and the kings and the generals.

SOCRATES These men are not elected, not chosen by the people?

PAUSANIAS No, we have a much better system. A small group of men
take the whole burden of the government on themselves, so
that the average citizen never has to worry about it at all.

SOCRATES Why, this gets better and better. The governing class does
the worrying for everybody?

PAUSANIAS Yes, all of it.

SOCRATES But then it does all the burdensome thinking in every field?

PAUSANIAS Yes, true.

SOCRATES And the ordinary man's thoughts are rationed out to him
just like his clothes and food?

PAUSANIAS Even so.

SOCRATES And the ephors and kings and generals are so conscientious
and self-sacrificing that they live on the same plain rations
that are given to the workmen and soldiers?

PAUSANIAS They usually have some property.

SOCRATES Oh, they do not live on the same plain scale as the workmen?

PAUSANIAS No. They deserve more and naturally they receive more than
the commoners.

SOCRATES And how do they keep their places? Is there sometimes
violence among them, a murder now and then when property
or power is concentrated unfairly in the hands of a few?

PAUSANIAS It's been known to happen.

SOCRATES It happens rather often?

PAUSANIAS Rather often.

SOCRATES Then what you have is a governing class of freebooters and murderers, holding the population down by terror and strict controls?

PAUSANIAS We don't starve a man's children because he has no money! That's brutal!

SOCRATES Murder is more merciful?

PAUSANIAS Far more! It's quick, neat, and practically painless. It's the ideal death. Starvation, that's slow torture! Inhuman!

SOCRATES Let us worry about that. Give us back our democracy!

PAUSANIAS If I hadn't worried about you a little you'd be lying out there in a ditch and Critias would still be walking around.

SOCRATES Was that why you plucked him green?

PAUSANIAS It was.

SOCRATES You lost money by murdering him too soon?

PAUSANIAS A pot of it.

SOCRATES You're not consistent, O King! Why should you lose money to save my worthless neck?

PAUSANIAS That's my weakness. I like a man, I like to keep him alive.

XANTIPPE [Going to Pausanias] You're only pretending you're a fool!

PAUSANIUS Woman, do you want to ruin me?

XANTIPPE Anyway, I do know something good about you.

PAUSANIAS Well, that's possible.
[SATYROS looks in at the door]
God, what an ugly mug! What have you done with Critias?

SATYROS Laid him in his house.

PAUSANIAS And where's the money?

SATYROS   Aboard your trireme.

PAUSANIAS How much?

SATYROS   We thought it was safer not to count it. It's loaded in the
hold—in the original bags. A hundred and four of them, each
marked "one talent."

PAUSANIAS Not what I hoped for, but it will do. And where are the
occupation forces?

SATYROS   They've left the Acropolis. They're marching toward the
ships.

PAUSANIAS You may go.
[SATYROS *leaves*]
One thing further I must tell you, Socrates. I make it my
business to know what people are thinking. I have to. If
Athens goes back to being a democracy you won't be safe
here. You'll be tried on that same old charge they nailed up
against you once before. And if it comes to a vote you could
be found guilty. So choose some honest, stupid man, with no
more brain than I have, and in he shall go as despot here.
And choose a friend of yours. You may need protection.

SOCRATES I rather like you, Stupid. You have the endearing qualities of
the frankly criminal class—but the courts are my protection.

PAUSANIAS I'm quite serious about it. Let me put a friend of yours in
here, and let him do a little quiet looting for you, for if any
trouble comes up the first thing a man needs is money.

SOCRATES I've never needed money.

PAUSANIAS Then you've never been in trouble.

XANTIPPE We've always needed money.

SOCRATES Not stolen money.

XANTIPPE I wouldn't mind how we got it!

SOCRATES Stupid's notion of quiet looting is to send some quiet experts to the homes of the well to do, strangle the latter from behind without outcry and take over their money and property.

PAUSANIAS I don't mind what you think about me, you know. I'm just a stupid king, and it doesn't matter what happens to me. But I'm concerned about you. Look, who was the greatest statesman you ever had in Athens?

SOCRATES Pericles, probably.

PAUSANIAS And who was his teacher?

SOCRATES Did he have a teacher, O Monarch?

PAUSANIAS You know, the one he studied philosophy and rhetoric and physics under. . . .

SOCRATES Anaxagoras?

PAUSANIAS That's it, Annex—what's-his-name. Now this Annex was a famous teacher and he charged for his lessons and he had the protection of the head of the state but he made one mistake. He said in public that the sun was not a god but a ball of fire—and what happened to him?

XANTIPPE He was exiled. Banished. By popular vote.

PAUSANIAS Right. He had a choice between drinking hemlock and getting out, and he got out. And then there was another -agoras, not Annex—you must have known him.

SOCRATES Protagoras. Yes, I knew him.

PAUSANIAS What happened to him?

THEODOTE He wrote a treatise on the gods, saying he didn't know whether they existed or not, and he was exiled, and he should have been!

PAUSANIAS By popular vote?

XANTIPPE He was tried before a jury of five hundred and found guilty of
irreligion.

PAUSANIAS You seem to think I'm pretty rough on the rich. Maybe I am,
but Athens has been pretty rough on philosophers. I understand that you too have said a few things about the gods.

SOCRATES And this worries you!

PAUSANIAS It worries me.

SOCRATES You choose the strangest things to worry about. I've spent
my life talking. It's possible that I've said a few things on
nearly every subject.

PAUSANIAS What you said about the gods is remembered. It's been
repeated to me.

SOCRATES I make my sacrifices in the temple daily.

PAUSANIAS Believing what?

SOCRATES Believing devoutly that no man knows where he came from
or what he should do while here or where he is going, and that
he should search without rest for the answers to these questions—in books and at the altars of the gods and in his own
mind.

PAUSANIAS It won't do. They'll have you up for it.

SOCRATES I hope they do have me up for it. Nothing could be healthier
than to bring the whole thing into the open, right out in the
good sunlight before every man in Athens, with every possible charge leveled against me and full discussion of politics,
gods, and men.

PAUSANIAS They'll get you, like they got those two agorasses—

SOCRATES Not Athens, not my city of Athens!

PAUSANIAS Well, I have to go. I'll have one of those bags of silver sent
to your house. I won't miss it, and it'll make you rich the
rest of your life—

SOCRATES   Don't send it. I don't want it.

XANTIPPE   Socrates!

SOCRATES   If it comes here I'll give it to the poor.

XANTIPPE   Where will you find anybody poorer than we are?

PAUSANIAS   We're always on the same side, aren't we, Xantippe? Well, farewell.

[THEODOTE *takes his arm and they turn toward the door.* CRITOBULUS *rushes in not seeing Pausanias*]

CRITOB.   Socrates! Critias has been killed!

SOCRATES   We thought you had gone to Piraeus.

CRITOB.   Yes—we were all going to join the rebellion against Critias, but the news caught up with us and they're all coming to Athens! Critias is dead and the Spartans are retreating to their ships and there's nobody between us and freedom except King Pausanias! He's hiding somewhere and we're going to find him and kill him!

[CRITO, LAMPROCLES, ANYTAS, CRASSOS, LYCON, *and* MELETOS *enter behind Critobulus*]

LAMPROC.   Father! We've won! The revolution has won! We're going to search every house till we find Pausanias and kill him! Come in, come in! Groups of our army are searching the houses they know best! Come in!

SOCRATES   Why, yes, come in, all of you, and greetings—but I think it won't be necessary to kill King Pausanias.

LYCON   There's the king! He's here!

[*He whips out his dagger and leaps at Pausanias, who has drawn his sword.* SOCRATES *stops Lycon*]

SOCRATES   Gently, Lycon.

LYCON   Do you defend him? Then this is for you!

           [*He draws back his arm to strike but* CRASSOS *catches it*]

CRASSOS   Father—would you kill Socrates?

LYCON   Yes, I would kill Socrates!

SOCRATES   [*Taking the dagger from Lycon's hand*] That also may be
           unnecessary, my dear Lycon. In fact, this entire revolution
           might be concluded without killing anybody. If we put our
           case to King Pausanias he could probably be persuaded to
           sheath his sword and re-establish Athenian democracy and go
           home.

PAUSANIAS Do you still wish democracy re-established in Athens?

SOCRATES   Of course I do!

PAUSANIAS The old charge will be brought up against you. You will go on
           trial for your life.

SOCRATES   Then I shall be tried in open court, Pausanias. It's our way of
           achieving justice under our peculiar system.

PAUSANIAS In my opinion you are unlikely to receive justice.

SOCRATES   I shall accept whatever verdict the jury reaches.

PAUSANIAS Very well! Don't say I didn't warn you!
           [*He turns to the crowd*]
           So you think you have a revolution here? You're welcome to
           it! You're welcome to this pesthole and your methods of
           running it. Put up your blades and I'll cover mine. One, two,
           three.
           [*Nobody moves*]
           Listen, I'll count three again, and this time if you don't put
           away those knives some people are going to die here—and I
           won't be the first. One, two, three.
           [*Swords and daggers are sheathed simultaneously*]
           It's a pleasure. Never fight unless you have to.

SOCRATES   Now I suggest that we form a guard of honor and conduct the king to the Senate, where he will formally surrender possession of the city into the hands of its citizens.

ANYTAS   A guard of honor? He's our prisoner.

MELETOS   He's our prisoner and he's under guard!

SOCRATES   It's hard to tell the difference between a police guard and guard of honor. But let's escort him. Otherwise some hothead might murder him before he goes through the ceremony.

CRITO   That's very true. We'll form an escort. Lead the way, Meletos.

[*The men go out, escorting the king.* XANTIPPE *looks at Theodote*]

XANTIPPE   Are you going south with the king?

THEODOTE   He's forgotten about me.

[*She sits*]

XANTIPPE   We're both forgotten.

THEODOTE   You're a wife. Yours will come back.

XANTIPPE   Out of habit, perhaps.

[*She sits*]

THEODOTE   It's better than trying to be seductive every day. I don't feel seductive every day.

XANTIPPE   Theodote?

THEODOTE   Yes, Xantippe.

XANTIPPE   Sometimes when I'm near you I smell one perfume, sometimes another, and sometimes a mingling of perfumes. Why is that?

THEODOTE   I use more than one. In different places.

XANTIPPE Does it—do men . . . like it?

THEODOTE They're mad about perfumes. They go sniffing and snuffing
and hunting and getting more and more excited till . . .

[*She pauses*]

XANTIPPE What kinds do you use? You don't mind telling me?

THEODOTE Of course not. Palm oil on the face and breast, marjoram on
the eyebrows and hair, oil of thyme on the ears and knees,
mint on the arms, myrrh on the legs and feet. And on the
thighs—

XANTIPPE Yes?

THEODOTE I have my own preparation for the thighs. I could lend you
some.

XANTIPPE What was there between you and Socrates?

THEODOTE Not much. Something. Long ago. But it was Alcibiades I
loved. And he's dead. . . . Sometimes I like to see Socrates
because he was Alcibiades' friend. Do you mind?

XANTIPPE No. Marjoram on the hair, thyme on the throat and knees?

THEODOTE Yes.

XANTIPPE Am I a fool to be in love when I'm old?

THEODOTE What better is there to do, old or young?

XANTIPPE Yes.
[*She looks out the door*]
What better?

CURTAIN

Act Two

Act Two

SCENE I

SCENE: *The house of Socrates a few days or weeks later. Socrates, Xantippe, Lamprocles, and Phoenix are seated at the breakfast table.* LYSIS *runs in to join them.*

LYSIS   I'm sorry I'm late! We were running races and—oh!

          [*He leaps up, combing his fingers through his hair*]

XANTIPPE What is it now?

LYSIS   I came through the bushes and I must have got some kind of bug in my hair. There it is—on the table.

LAMPROC. It looks like a tick. Shall I kill it?

XANTIPPE Not on the table, please!

LAMPROC. Well, don't let it get away. It does look like a tick.

LYSIS   I'm watching it. It can't get away.

          [*The boys follow its progress across the table, fascinated*]

LAMPROC. It's got a small head.
          [*He touches it*]
          And a hard shell.

LYSIS   It could be just a plain harmless little beetle.

PHOENIX   Shall I crunch him?

XANTIPPE No! Not on the table!

SOCRATES Why don't we give him a fair trial? If he's a tick, kill him. If he's a plain harmless little beetle let him off. That's the Athenian way.

XANTIPPE I wish you wouldn't joke about trials.

57

SOCRATES   Why not, Xantippe? A fair trial for the accused is the heart of our political system. A man isn't guilty till he's found guilty. And neither is a bug.

XANTIPPE   But why must they try you now? There's plenty to do just to re-establish the democracy and clean up after the way things were under the Thirty! Why don't they just do that?

SOCRATES   I don't know, Xantippe, but I do know that history doesn't come at us the way it should. It comes at us any old way, higgledy-piggledy, and every day when you look at it it looks like a mess. The next day a new mess is poured on top of the old mess, and nothing is ever cleaned up. The whole thing stratifies and petrifies down below, so underneath it's a petrified mess and on top it's a fresh mess and it goes on that way forever.

LAMPROC.   I maintain that this is not a six-legged fellow at all, but an eight-legger! Ticks have eight legs and no wings! It's a tick!

LYSIS   I maintain that he's a warmhearted and gentle little beetle, with six legs and nothing to bite with!

PHOENIX   It's a six-legger! I counted them!

LYSIS   Innocent! Not a tick!

LAMPROC.   All right, I don't accuse it of being a tick! I accuse it of being a female Athenian under thirty and guilty of violating the sumptuary law governing the rules of dress! It is not wearing its chiton in such fashion as to expose one leg as far as the thigh.

[*The boys lean over to examine the bug closely*]

XANTIPPE   Is there truly such a law?

SOCRATES   There is. There have been too many unmarried girls and too many bachelors since the war ended. Maybe they couldn't afford marriage, or thought they couldn't. So three days

ago this statute became effective, and every girl on the street
slips along with one leg twinkling.

LYSIS   Oh, oh. It's gone.

[*They look for the bug unsuccessfully*]

PHOENIX   It wasn't guilty anyway. It was showing all six legs. Up to
its bottom.

XANTIPPE   Is there no law against showing too much?

LAMPROC.   Yes, there is, but that's an old law. Nobody bothers about
that. It's this new law that's causing all the excitement.

SOCRATES   What kind of excitement?

LAMPROC.   Oh, soldiers whistling and calling out after girls, and girls
pulling at their clothes and blushing and hurrying by.

SOCRATES   Here's somebody who can tell us about it. Come in, Theodote.
What's the mood of the streets?

[THEODOTE *enters*]

THEODOTE   Greetings! Greetings to the table and the house! You should
see the streets! Perhaps the girls were a little bashful at first,
but today you should see them! Every vendable maid in
Athens is being walked up and down by her mother, her best
leg foremost. Those with good legs show a good deal, those
with so-so legs show a misleading trace, those with bad legs
have found ways of draping the material so that a man might
think if she brings a little money these legs are not so bad.

XANTIPPE   And the men?

THEODOTE   Oh, the men walk up and down and gape as if such wonders
had never been seen! Girls are going like hot cakes. There
have never been so many troths plighted in a morning since
legs were first invented.

XANTIPPE   This has destroyed your business, no doubt?

THEODOTE Oh, no—licit and illicit business have improved together!

XANTIPPE Theodote!

THEODOTE Yes, my dear Xantippe.

XANTIPPE You too are wearing this open dress prescribed by law.

THEODOTE Of course.

[*She exhibits her drapery*]

XANTIPPE But the law applies to maids under thirty!

THEODOTE Every single woman is a maiden, naturally. And what woman is over thirty?

XANTIPPE I am.

THEODOTE Then you're the first I've known. But I'm not here to talk about this. King Pausanias is coming to Athens.

XANTIPPE For the trial?

THEODOTE No, he's coming to see me.

LAMPROC. The king of Sparta?

THEODOTE I know it's incredible, but listen. This morning a messenger arrived at my house and asked for Theodote. I said that I was Theodote. He said that he brought a message for me from the king of Sparta. I asked to see it and he said that the king of Sparta did not write. He then delivered himself thus: "The king sends greetings to Theodote and wishes her to know that the rations of Sparta are tasteless after the viands of Athens. The king will see Theodote soon and she will prepare herself for a journey." End quote.

XANTIPPE You're to return to Sparta with him!

THEODOTE It can mean nothing else.

LAMPROC. Does this happen to kings, too?

SOCRATES Oh, when the bright stroke falls it can blind kings like the rest of us. But we shall have a friend at court.

THEODOTE While I'm there. I don't expect it to last forever. He has a wife for official purposes. I'm a half-breed and strictly unofficial.

LYSIS Will you live in a palace?

THEODOTE Some part of a palace, I suppose. Or maybe one wing of a palace.

LYSIS And will you have servants?

THEODOTE Countless servants. All Lacedemon will rush to help me into my chariot. There will be great bronze mirrors and barrels of oil and hogsheads of beauty creams.

XANTIPPE You're to be the companion of a king and have everything. [*She looks round her room*] I hate you.

THEODOTE You shall have your old Silenus all to yourself.

XANTIPPE I've never had anything. I hate you.

SOCRATES Why, Xantippe, do you envy Theodote?

XANTIPPE Yes, I do!

SOCRATES But what have we ever needed that we haven't had?

XANTIPPE Riches! Great riches!

SOCRATES My dear wife, you're speaking out in quite a new way. What would we want with great riches?

XANTIPPE All right, I'll speak out in a new way, and for once I'll say what I think! Everybody goes around praising temperance and moderation and poverty and all that nonsense! You go around praising them—you most of all! And nobody wants them—nobody! What people want is luxuries, and loads of money, and loads of everything, and people waiting on them —and that's what I want! You're always looking for the honest truth and there it is! People don't want to be poor. They want to have everything, and so do I!

SOCRATES   Of course, not everybody can have everything.

XANTIPPE   Of course not! Let them do without. I've done without long enough! Let other people try it. How many do you know that aren't trying to get rich or stay rich or climb out of the hole they're in? I only know one, and that's you! One man in all the world! And, God help me, it just happens to be my priceless luck to be married to that one man.

SOCRATES   You say it well, Xantippe. I have never heard such a clear and passionate statement of the position. The only trouble is that you don't mean it. . . .

XANTIPPE   Don't mean it?

SOCRATES   If you had Theodote's chance you wouldn't take it.

XANTIPPE   When offered servants and a palace?

SOCRATES   You would think the matter over for a few days and in the end you would decide to remain here and eke out an existence on the same three obols a day—

XANTIPPE   That's what you would do!

SOCRATES   Think how we'd waste those three obols if you weren't here.

XANTIPPE   [*A bit shaken*] The spending of the money I'd turn over to Lysis. He has some sense—

THEODOTE   And so far you haven't received any offers.

XANTIPPE   True. And I won't.

LAMPROC.   We have visitors.

          [He goes to usher in Phaedo and Crito]

SOCRATES   Crito! Phaedo! Come in. We are discussing the advantages
of wealth over poverty.

XANTIPPE   Poverty wins, of course.

CRITO   We looked for you at the banker's tables, but you weren't
there, so—

PHAEDO   We wanted to talk over some preparations for the trial—
nothing difficult—just things that have to be done.

CRITO   And since it's not far off—the trial, I mean—they should
be seen to while there's time.

XANTIPPE   Boys, we're in the way.

CRITO   No, you're not, Xantippe. It's usual in trials that involve
the death penalty that the wife and children of the defendant
appear with him and ask for clemency. We must arrange
where you will stand and when you will approach the judges'
seats.

THEODOTE   I'm not needed here, I think.

PHAEDO   No, only the family.

THEODOTE   I'll join the parade of calves and men.

          [She goes out]

PHOENIX   Are we to go to the trial?

LYSIS   It looks that way.

CRITO   Since there are no places reserved it occurred to us that we
two could go early and take Xantippe and the boys with us.
And there'd be some prearranged signal for them to come
forward. Would this suit you, Xantippe?

XANTIPPE Whatever you say.

PHAEDO The trial's to begin in the morning and it may last some time, so we'll bring something to eat and drink.

XANTIPPE I'll get the boys ready early. We'll have to wear what we have on. There's nothing else.

PHAEDO All the better. It's well to give the impression that you are not well to do.

XANTIPPE We can give that impression.

CRITO It's usual, even, to borrow tattered cloaks for the whole family and rehearse a scene of weeping which you will play out at the trial—before the magistrates and the jurors.

SOCRATES This we can't do, Crito.

CRITO Have you ever attended a serious trial where it was not done?

SOCRATES No.

CRITO When you come into a court you have to do what is customary. Otherwise the court and the jury feel that you are not paying them due respect, and they resent it.

SOCRATES If it were customary to bribe the jurors would you expect me to do that, too?

CRITO Socrates, if bribery were customary you would have to do that, too. Luckily you're spared that.

PHAEDO There's one other matter that has to be attended to, and that's the preparation of the defense. There's a rhetorician, Zephyros, who has conducted thirty-four cases before the great court in the past two years and has not lost one case. Now, we don't want anything to go wrong, Socrates. It's so easy to make a legal slip and deliver yourself over to your enemies. Let us bring Zephyros into this, at least for consultation. He'd be willing to do that for you.

SOCRATES   If we need the children we'll call you, Xantippe.

XANTIPPE   Yes.

           [XANTIPPE *and the three boys go out*]

SOCRATES   Phaedo, Crito, we have attended many trials together where
           we listened to prepared speeches—read by the defendant but
           written by a rhetorician—and we have watched the weeping
           of families, too, rehearsed and staged to move the hearts of
           the jurors. In most cases the men were acquitted when these
           things were well carried out. But unless I'm mistaken there's
           always some sly perversion of the truth in a professional
           defense, even if it were not a slight misrepresentation, though
           accepted, that one man should write words for another. And
           when it comes to the public grieving of the accused man's
           family, that's really an attempt to corrupt the court. For
           the jurors should judge him according to the evidence and
           with no thought of his family.

CRITO   But the vote may go against you if you fail to make these
           traditional gestures.

SOCRATES   Would you think better of me or worse of me if I allowed
           Xantippe and my sons to wail for me on a public platform?

CRITO   It's the jury I'm worried about, not me.

SOCRATES   But it's you I'm worried about, not the jury—you and
           Phaedo and the rest of my friends—and myself. Would my
           friends and I think better of me or worse for these tricks?
           Answer truthfully.

CRITO   Not better. And still I think you should use them.

SOCRATES   Not better—worse. And that answers you.

PHAEDO   But this trial is serious, Socrates.

SOCRATES   What could be more serious than how well my friends think
           of me? Nothing, I should say.

CRITO   When you speak in public you probe into things—and that's
           exactly what Anytas and the others accuse you of—and
           you're very likely to give a demonstration that will convince
           the jury of your guilt.

           [XANTIPPE *comes to the inner door and listens*]

SOCRATES   You see, Crito, I am accused of being the kind of man who
           corrupts and falsifies and distorts and destroys. Now if I
           am that kind of man I should be put out of the way. But how
           can the jury tell what kind of man I am if I go before them
           speaking words that are not mine and hiding behind a crying
           wife and children? Do you think they are likely to think me
           guilty if they see me as I am?

CRITO   Not likely to think you guilty, but likely to find you guilty.
           And I myself, Socrates, am not sure why you refuse to take
           advantage of these devices all men use. You're involved here
           in a matter of life and death. Isn't it a little pretentious of
           you to say: "I'll do it my own way and they'll have to take
           me as I am"?

SOCRATES   Pretentious? Now what does it pretend to? There are some
           customs in our courts which make me uncomfortable when
           other men use them. If I tried to use them they'd make me so
           uncomfortable that I couldn't go on. I just don't want to be
           uncomfortable.

PHAEDO   There are things even less comfortable.

SOCRATES   Are there? Maybe we're not being quite honest . . . on
           either side. You're concerned about me, and I'm grateful for
           that, and you're trying to save me from my own bullheaded-
           ness—but it can't be done. It can't be done because I look
           forward to this trial as an athlete looks forward to the race
           he has longed for, as a wrestler looks forward to the bout for
           which all his life has been a training. All my life I've been
           accused of things and I've never been able to answer back.
           Day after tomorrow is my day! Let another man write the
           words I'm to say? Never! It's my day! And I go toward it
           with a very light heart, Crito. I don't know why Anytas and

Meletos insist on pressing that old indictment against me, but whatever their motives they couldn't have pleased me more.

CRITO   You will speak extempore, as you always speak?

SOCRATES   Offhand, as always.

CRITO   And you expect to succeed?

SOCRATES   Mind you, I know, at my age, how dusty success is. And yet there's a kind of dew on it, too. The morning of the trial will have dew over it—and I shall walk through it and revel in it. Don't be angry with me.

CRITO   No, but I must go.

PHAEDO   And I must.

CRITO   And I see that you must do it your own way.

SOCRATES   No question. But I do thank you. Remain my friends.

PHAEDO   No question of that.

CRITO   None. And we'll see you?

SOCRATES   I'd go with you only there was something I wanted to do at home first.
[*He looks round him*]
I'll remember it in a moment.

CRITO   At the market, then.

SOCRATES   At the market.
[CRITO *and* PHAEDO *go out.* SOCRATES *follows them to the door, then turns and looks about, trying to remember. His eye falls on Xantippe*]
Yes, of course. That's what it was.

XANTIPPE   I wanted to tell you—I think you're wrong—I think one might just as well give up and have things like the rest of the world. But that doesn't mean I don't love you. I do.

Every once in a while I go a little mad on the subject of wanting things—because I've never had them, and I've always worked, and . . .

SOCRATES   In all history there's never been a husband so trying to the nerves of a wife.

XANTIPPE   In all history there's never been a wife so violent and disagreeable. Of course, I've had good reason most of the time.

SOCRATES   I think you have.

XANTIPPE   But—

SOCRATES   Yes?

XANTIPPE   Don't hate me.

SOCRATES   Whatever gave you that idea?

XANTIPPE   Do you know that it's—it's a long time since you've put your arms round me?

SOCRATES   Is it?

XANTIPPE   Yes.

SOCRATES   I remember that when I was young I worked something out in my mind . . . about people in love. It seemed to me that people making love were always getting into ridiculous positions—and yet they did get into them, and they didn't mind it—and the reason was that when you're young you have violent passions, and you also have the excuse that the whole ridiculous business is necessary because without it there'd be no children. But when you get old . . . your passions—you have them but they're not so violent—and you don't have that excuse of possible children. Maybe this gets in my way a little.

XANTIPPE   It gets in my way, too.

SOCRATES   So—what do we do?

XANTIPPE   When I go to the trial I want to watch you and remember
            that you love me a little.

SOCRATES   You can do that easily, Xantippe. Our sons will sit with you.

XANTIPPE   Would you, before the trial, lie with your head in my lap the
            way you did long ago—and I'll sit and look into the distance
            and think of what it was all like then?

SOCRATES   Yes. Of course it's morning.

XANTIPPE   Tonight will do as well.

SOCRATES   But why not in the morning? Sometimes it's good to break
            precedents

XANTIPPE   I have work to do.

SOCRATES   Well, so have I, but sit and let's try how it is.
            [*She sits. He lies with his head in her lap. She looks into the
            distance and strokes his hair*]
            By the dog, I almost feel young! When did you take to wear-
            ing perfumes?

XANTIPPE   Only lately. Do you like it?

SOCRATES   Yes, I rather like it. Do you know what I have a mind to do?

XANTIPPE   No.

SOCRATES   I have a mind to say a prayer.

XANTIPPE   You used to say a prayer to the god Pan when you lay thus
            long ago.

SOCRATES   Will the children come back?

XANTIPPE   No, I saw to that.

SOCRATES   Beloved Pan, and all you other gods who haunt this city,
            give me beauty in the inward soul, for outward beauty I'm

not likely to have. May I reckon the wise to be the wealthy and those who need least to be most like the gods.

XANTIPPE It's the same old prayer.

SOCRATES [*Continuing*] Make me content with what I have but not self-satisfied. Let me give more than I get, love more than I hate, and think more of living than of having lived. . . . Anything more? This prayer, I think, is enough for me.

[*She continues to stroke his hair, looking into the distance*]

END OF SCENE

Act Two

SCENE: *We are in the middle of the trial. The audience in the theater is now the jury of five hundred and Anytas is concluding his speech to them. On the stage a magistrate sits listening, ready to make rulings. Socrates sits near him, and, on the other side, Meletos. Xantippe and the three sons are near the judge but not among the speakers. Theodote and King Pausanias are seen, but not part of the trial itself. Crito and Phaedo are somewhere visible.*

ANYTAS   We have accused Socrates on three counts. First, he teaches a new religion, with gods of his own devising, and casts out the old gods of Greece from his atheistic temple. For the truth is that he believes in no gods at all, and has no belief, and is not even sure that the earth is here and men are walking on it. Second, he corrupts the young men of our city by cynically questioning all the precepts and patterns of conduct by which we have lived since the time of Solon. Third, by some fatality which cannot be chance, all the greatest enemies of Athens, those who have done her the most damage by means of treason, ill counsel, and demagoguery, have been his pupils and friends. He has taken no part in our politics but they have. We are a beggar city now, disarmed, punished by the gods for disbelief, disbelief that had its origin in, and spread out from, the brain of one man. We ask for the death of this man. . . . As you know, he has the right to question us on all these points during the trial, and no doubt he will, for questioning is what he likes best. Of all the orators of our time he is the trickiest and most persuasive. Beware of him. Don't let him trick you or make the worse appear the better cause, for that is his vocation and he has done it all too well. He does it so well, and has done it so well for forty years, that he has dragged our city down with him into the compost heap of his own thought. We leave the verdict to you.

   [*He sits*]

MAGIS.   Socrates will now speak in his own defense.

71

SOCRATES   [*Rising, taking his place*] Men of Athens, if Anytas wished to
be believed he should never have said that I'm an orator, for
you'll soon discover that I'm not. I'm afraid you'll hear from
me only the first plain words that come to hand. I'm not used
to speaking from a platform and I've never before been in a
lawsuit. I'm a stranger to the language of this place. I shall
have to speak as I have always spoken in the streets. . . .
Now I am accused of ruining Athens, and those who accuse
me ask that I be put to death. They may be right, but let
me tell you how I became the kind of fellow I am. My father
was a sculptor—no, he was a stonecutter, and I took the
same trade and I was a stonecutter. There are some marbles
in the sanctuary of the Parthenon that I remember working
on. But I had what was known as a shrewd wit—a workman's
wit—and it was my habit to talk while I chiseled the stone. I
talked and cracked about politics and public affairs and
statesmen and kept the whole workroom in good humor. After
a while people began to drift into the factory to listen to me,
and the crowds around my bench were large enough to become a nuisance. The day arrived when I had to stop talking
or quit work, and so I moved my conversations into the street.
By this time I was nearly forty years of age, and married, and
my wife brought me a bit of money—not a fortune, three
obols a day—and talking to the men in the streets became my
work. And what did I talk about? Well, I'm afraid I was just
a joker at first, because it amused people, but I sometimes
joked about important men and questions, as we all do—and
it happened after a while that I met some of these important
men. Now I was only an irresponsible ignoramus, but I
began to find that I knew as much about many things as the
important people did. And I began to question them and
stick needles in them—and sometimes I showed them up
as ignoramuses—and they were angry. And I invented a sort
of question-and-answer game for getting people into corners,
and my following grew larger, because there's nothing people
like better than seeing public men confused and unable to
answer. I was just as unable to answer as they were, but I
was asking the questions, not answering them, and so I
acquired a reputation for wisdom which I didn't deserve and
don't deserve now. . . . The next thing that happened,
though, seemed to me very serious. A friend of mine, now
dead, a man well known to many of you, named Chairephon,

went to Delphi and had the audacity to ask the oracle if there were any wiser man than Socrates. And the priestess answered no. This was heard by many citizens and when the news came to me I was stunned, for I had never pretended to wisdom and still don't. Yet I couldn't help taking the matter seriously and I asked myself, "What can the god mean?" For a long while I was at a loss, but then I decided to continue my question-and-answer game, testing every man I met till I found somebody wiser than myself. And that search has gone on from that day to this, making me many enemies, no doubt, among those who were stumped by my questions, and getting me just about nowhere. I have not found one man who knows what holiness is, or wisdom, or courage or loyalty or faith. And I still don't know. I have put in a lifetime of Herculean labor to prove the god wrong, and I have not proved him either wrong or right.

MELETOS   Do you deny that you questioned the existence of the gods?

MAGIS.   Let us be orderly, Meletos!

SOCRATES   [*To the judge*] This I can answer now, sir. Meletos, I am nearly seventy years old. In the course of the last thirty or forty years I have asked questions on nearly every subject. By the dog, I have not spared anything or anybody, myself included, and if matters of religion ever came up for discussion I pursued my usual course. It has been my fixed principle that the uncovering of truth could do no harm. I have believed that questioning could injure only what is false among workmen, businessmen, Sophists, statesmen or gods. The air of a democracy is only healthy when inquiry bites constantly at the heels of every proposal and every project, even at the foundations of our way of life.

MELETOS   You have bitten into them and you have destroyed them!

SOCRATES   May I ask you a question, Meletos?

MELETOS   No.

SOCRATES   Will the magistrate instruct Meletos to answer?

MAGIS.   You must answer him, Meletos.

MELETOS   Very well.

SOCRATES   Do you believe the truth can do harm?

MELETOS   No.

SOCRATES   Do you believe free discussion can do harm?

MELETOS   No.

SOCRATES   Then you would oppose censorship?

MELETOS   I would.

SOCRATES   But I am a citizen of Athens. Would you impose censorship
           on me?

MELETOS   I would. On you alone.

SOCRATES   But if there were another man like me you would apply it to
           him?

MELETOS   Yes, I would!

SOCRATES   And if there were twenty like us you would apply it to all
           twenty?

MELETOS   Yes, I would!

SOCRATES   And if I had pupils who spoke like me you would apply it to
           them?

MELETOS   Yes!

SOCRATES   Do you put any limit on the number you would censor if they
           agreed with me?

MELETOS   No!

SOCRATES   But a moment ago you said you would oppose censorship,
           and now you say you would enforce it!

MELETOS   I would enforce censorship on people like you!

SOCRATES   What kind of people would that be, Meletos?

MELETOS   People who don't believe in the gods! You don't believe in
           them. You've sometimes been heard praying or sacrificing to
           demigods or to the god Pan or to your own private demon,
           but the central gods of Athens you never mention!

SOCRATES   But I do believe in demigods?

MELETOS   You've been heard praying to them!

SOCRATES   Meletos, it is known that mules are the offspring of horses
           and asses. Could a man believe in mules without believing
           that horses and asses exist?

MELETOS   Hardly.

SOCRATES   It is also known that demigods are the offspring of gods and
           mortals. Could a man believe in demigods without believing
           that the gods exist?

ANYTAS   There! You hear it! You all hear it! He compares the mating
           of gods and mortals to the mating of horses and donkeys.
           And he compares demigods to mules!

SOCRATES   Do you see no similarity, Anytas?

ANYTAS   I see an impious man before me, and that's what we came to
           prove.

SOCRATES   Tell me, Anytas, do the words in our language have definite
           meanings, or do the meanings shift about?

ANYTAS   They have definite meanings, you will find!

SOCRATES   Do you know the meanings of our words?

ANYTAS   I do!

SOCRATES   Of all our words?

ANYTAS   I think so.

SOCRATES   What a fortunate man! Here I have been trying all these
            years to find the meaning of three or four, and they con-
            stantly elude me. But then you know the meaning of the
            words in the indictment you have signed against me?

ANYTAS   I do, indeed.

SOCRATES   What is the meaning of the word impious?

ANYTAS   [*To the judge*] Must we go through this rigmarole?

MAGIS.   You must answer. It is the law.

ANYTAS   Impious means not serving the gods, not believing in them.

SOCRATES   And what does pious mean—pious, I believe, being the
            opposite of impious?

ANYTAS   It means serving the gods and believing in them.

SOCRATES   Does it mean both these things?

ANYTAS   It means both these things!

            [*He turns away in disgust*]

SOCRATES   Please follow me closely, Anytas, and don't despise these
            questions, for they truly have a reason. If to be pious is both
            to believe in the gods and to serve them, is it possible for
            one man to believe in the gods but not serve them and for
            another man to serve them without believing in them?

ANYTAS   This is an asinine question!

SOCRATES   But is it possible?

ANYTAS   It is possible, yes.

SOCRATES   Now if one man served the gods without knowing much about
            them, while another man knew them very well but failed to
            serve them, which would deserve punishment?

ANYTAS   Must I answer this silliness, too?

MAGIS.   Yes.

SOCRATES   Is not he who serves the gods the more righteous man?

ANYTAS   Perhaps.

SOCRATES   Not perhaps, Anytas. What is your honest opinion? One believes in the gods but does not serve them, the other has some doubts but serves them. Which should be punished.

[*A pause*]

MELETOS   He who believes in the gods but does not serve them is the guilty man!

SOCRATES   Thank you, Meletos. And he is the more guilty, is he not, because he has great faith in them and still does not do their bidding?

MELETOS   He is.

SOCRATES   But now a difficulty arises. Has anyone among us been told face to face by the gods what they wish him to do?

MELETOS   No.

SOCRATES   And the rules for living laid down by the gods are rather general, are they not, so that a man must consider them carefully and weigh them well before he can be sure that his actions are such as the gods would approve?
[*Meletos is silent*]
You don't agree?

MELETOS   No.

SOCRATES   But you considered carefully before you brought this action against me?

MELETOS   Yes.

SOCRATES   Did you consult an oracle or receive any sign from the gods?
            Any of you three.

MELETOS   No.

            [*There is a pause.* SOCRATES *looks round, steps forward*]

SOCRATES   Men of Athens, I am a man of doubt, as my accusers have
            said. All my wisdom is in knowing how little I know. None of
            my questions has been answered, none of the definitions I
            sought has been found. We live our lives, it seems to me, in
            such mystery and darkness that I was quick to take the one
            hint I thought might have come my way from a god, the
            answer made by the Delphic Apollo to a question about
            myself. Since that answer I have continued to seek, sometimes
            gaily, sometimes ironically, but always seriously, for some-
            body wiser than I am. Perhaps I was wrong, but this is the
            closest I have ever come to hearing a mandate from any god,
            and I wished to do as the god directed. You see before you
            then, a man who is not sure of his faith but has tried hard to
            serve Apollo, and in his accusers you see men of complete
            faith who have not heard even a hint as to whether they are
            serving the gods or only themselves. By Meletos' own ad-
            mission these men are more guilty than I.

ANYTAS   But not by my admission!

MELETOS   And not by mine!

ANYTAS   Yes, you did admit it, you addlehead, and I warned you to be
            quiet—

MELETOS   Oh, you warned me!

MAGIS.   Gentlemen, you will address the jury and not each other.

SOCRATES   Yes, gentlemen. I would not wish you to lose this case un-
            fairly, and if you squabble among yourselves—

ANYTAS   Then answer this one fair question. Do you believe in the
            gods?

SOCRATES   Of course I do, Anytas.

ANYTAS   In all of them, or only some?

SOCRATES   In all of them, and many more than you do.

ANYTAS   Gods of your own, no doubt?

SOCRATES   No, no, gods of your own, Anytas. I believe in every god you have in mind, and in the gods as they seem in the mind of Meletos, and in the gods as Homer imagined them—

ANYTAS   Are not these the same gods?

SOCRATES   Is your mind exactly like the mind of Meletos?

ANYTAS   No, thank Zeus, it is not!

SOCRATES   Then the gods he conceives will be everywhere a little different from the gods of your thinking—

ANYTAS   I am not asking about the gods that are in anybody's mind. I am asking about the gods as they are on Mount Olympos!

SOCRATES   From whom did you learn about the gods on Olympos?

ANYTAS   From Homer, atheist!

SOCRATES   And from whom did Homer learn about them?

ANYTAS   From whom— Men of Athens, you hear him! He asks where Homer learned about the gods!

SOCRATES   But that's a very natural question, friend Anytas. Homer was a poet, and he wrote gloriously, as only a great poet can write. But were not the gods he wrote about the gods as he imagined them? And when he heard about them from others were they not somewhat different? Does not a great poet transmute what comes to him as bare fact and shadowy legend into a coherent and moving story?

ANYTAS   Do you believe the gods of Olympos to be sure and solid and real?

SOCRATES   As sure and solid and real as anything in this world!

[*Anytas pauses.* MELETOS *leaps up, speaks to Anytas*]

MELETOS   And that stops you, I think! [*To Socrates*] Only how sure and real is this world?

SOCRATES   Yes, how sure is it, Meletos? How sure are you that you are there questioning me? How sure are you that I am here replying? I have often wondered. I think the gods are just as real as we are, Meletos. Isn't that real enough?

MELETOS   Answer me! I ask it again. How real is this world?

SOCRATES   Of different degrees of reality, Meletos. Sometimes it seems to me that the gods in the pages of Homer are vividly alive, and that by comparison they are shadowy and indistinct on Mount Olympos. Sometimes it seems to me that your figure and mine, speaking here, are shadowy and indistinct, and will be quickly forgotten, while the scene of this trial, remembered and written down, say by young Plato there, who is always writing things down, may come vividly alive and remain so for a long time. Which then would be the more real, Meletos, the vivid scene written down or the shadowy one that actually takes place and then drifts away from men's minds and is lost?

[*Socrates pauses. Meletos pauses*]

ANYTAS   [*To Meletos*] And now I hope you're satisfied, now that he's sunk us all together in this bog of reality and unreality—

MELETOS   You didn't do so well with him, either!

ANYTAS   Why must you leap in and interrupt?

SOCRATES   It's the business of the young to interrupt their elders, Anytas. You and I are not so young any more, and we must expect to be interrupted from now on.

[ANYTAS *and* MELETOS *start to walk away in opposite directions.* LYCON *comes forward*]

MAGIS.   Who will continue with the prosecution?

ANYTAS   I will, if Meletos will be quiet!

MELETOS   I will, if Anytas can hold his tongue!

ANYTAS   It's better to say nothing than for you to talk!

MELETOS   Then we say nothing!

MAGIS.   Lycon, will you continue?

LYCON   I had hoped to remain in the background, sir, but now I have
          no choice. Citizens of Athens, you see what happens when
          you deal with this jester on his own terms. I shall not fall into
          that error. I have one plain point to make. Since the begin-
          ning of the Peloponnesian War our city has been led by the
          pupils of Socrates. Alcibiades was the evil spirit of Athens for
          twenty years, guiding us from one calamity to another.
          Socrates was his teacher! Charmides led the rebellion that
          overthrew our democracy and set up the unscrupulous
          Thirty. Socrates was his teacher! Critias completed the wreck
          of Athens which the other two had begun. Socrates was his
          teacher! Socrates taught all three a devilish ingenuity in
          logic which worked on men like a magic and led them to
          destroy themselves. These three were his chief followers, but
          there has been a whole rabble of others, the worst men of
          three generations, a volcano of corrupting fire and ash and
          lava, destroying our lives, our state, and our beliefs. And here
          he stands still—this monster who has let loose all these evils
          on us! Here he stands, in his hypocritical poverty, playing
          with words, pretending that he meant only good. He has
          brought death to so many of our young warriors that the
          cemeteries of our city have doubled in size in his lifetime. And
          he meant well! Oh, my brothers! Oh, the dead children of the
          long war—this man meant well!

SOCRATES Does it escape you, Lycon, that you have not shown a con-
          nection between my words and these disasters?

LYCON   Yet there is a connection, Socrates! There is a connection,
          citizens. [To Socrates] This little question-and-answer game

which you play at the bidding of Apollo, this game is not so
harmless as you pretend. It's a murderous weapon, this little
game! You point it at patriotism and it degenerates into
treason. You point it at a soldier and he begins to wonder
why he should fight for his country. You turn it on morals
and the robber begins to look like the honest man. You turn
it on the gods and suddenly the gods are puppets that some
fool imagined and set up long since on a barren mountain.
Your little game shakes all belief, makes the young men
question everything there is, and there are some matters a
nation must not question if it is to continue. It must not
question its virtues, its standards, its religion! If any city
questions these things it will wither away—its statesmen will
sell out, its warriors will break and run, its poets will cease
to sing, its women will turn toward the men of another nation
who still have faith in themselves! This is why your followers
have betrayed us . . . because you taught them corruption!

SOCRATES   Is it corruption to examine into the conditions of life?

LYCON   If you examine the beliefs by which men live you kill those
beliefs, and corruption follows.

SOCRATES   Should not beliefs die that will not stand examination?

LYCON   No! No belief will bear examination! Life will not bear it.
A tree cannot live if you look at its roots.

SOCRATES   This would be a very convenient rule for a tyrant or a dicta-
tor who did not wish to be examined, of course.

LYCON   But it's true—and you know it's true! You taught your
followers to believe in nothing, and you taught them the
sleight of hand by which they could lead others astray—and
you did this without fee—did it for sheer love of deviltry
and evil.

SOCRATES   Oh, come now, Lycon—

LYCON   I say you did! For pure love of evil, of destruction, of tearing
down! Out of hatred for Athens and its people and ways.

SOCRATES [*Angry for the first time*] You lie! I love Athens—and have always loved Athens—

LYCON Then why do you injure her?

SOCRATES [*To the magistrate*] Forgive me, sir! One should not grow angry in a court, and I have not been angry before, but when I hear it said that I have not loved Athens I cannot answer calmly! [*To Lycon*] And the thing I have loved most about my city is its freedom, its willingness to look at all the evidence there is and live in the same world with it.

LYCON Even if the evidence destroys it?

SOCRATES The evidence will not destroy a free city, Lycon. Far from destroying it, the truth will make and keep it free. A despotism dies of the truth, a democracy lives by it! And now I thank you for making me angry, for I realize something which had never been clear to me before. Athens has always seemed to me a sort of mad miracle of a city, flashing out in all directions, a great city for no discoverable reason. But now I see that Athens is driven and made miraculous by the same urge that has sent me searching your streets! It is the Athenian search for truth, the Athenian hunger for facts, the endless curiosity of the Athenian mind, that has made Athens unlike any other city. This is a city drenched with light—the light of frank and restless inquiry—and this light has flooded every corner of our lives: our courts, our theaters, our athletic games, our markets—even the open architecture of the temples of our gods! This has been our genius—a genius for light, for open hearings, for the uncovering of secret things; yes, for nakedness, for nakedness of the human body in the sun and for naked truth in the human mind! Shut out the light and close our minds and we shall be like a million cities of the past that came up out of mud, and worshiped darkness a little while, and went back, forgotten, into darkness!

[*He turns to Lycon*]

LYCON [*Somewhat subdued*] I shall ask one more question—one that you have so far evaded.

SOCRATES   Yes, Lycon.

LYCON   Was Alcibiades your friend?

SOCRATES   He was.

LYCON   Did he betray Athens?

SOCRATES   Not while he was my friend. Long after. And in justice to me,
Lycon, you must remember that when he betrayed Athens he
betrayed me, and betrayed my teachings. For he turned away
from us to serve a foreign tyrant. Perhaps freedom offers
temptations that some minds are not able to resist. When a
man is free he is free to choose wrong or right. In a free city
no man chooses for another. I did not choose for Alcibiades
or Charmides or Critias. I have chosen only for myself. For
myself I chose to fight for Athens at Potidaea and to walk
the streets of Athens seeking the truth.

LYCON   If you had to choose between Athens and the search for truth,
to which of these would you give your allegiance?

SOCRATES   They are one and the same, fortunately. Yet if you wish me to
say which I would choose if they were not the same—and I
see that you do wish it, Lycon—I must say that the search for
truth is more sacred than any god, more desirable than any
woman, more hopeful than any child, more lovely than any
city, even our own! [*To the jury*] If you have not seen this
you will vote against me, and you should. But you are men
of Athens, and you have seen it or Athens would not be here,
would not from the beginning have been possible! The unexamined life is not worth living! The unexamined life is
built on lies, and a free world cannot live by lies. Only a
world of slaves can live by lies!

LYCON   And so his allegiance is not to our city, but to the truth, the
phantom truth that he has never found. I think that is
enough. I leave the verdict to the men of Athens.

[*He walks off the stage.* SOCRATES *turns to the magistrate*]

MAGIS.   If there is no further argument we can now put the case to a
vote. The jurors will mark their ballots, and if they will then

keep their seats while the ballots are counted the outcome of
the trial will be announced.

[*There is some confusion on the stage.* PHAEDO *and* CRITO *climb
up on it, hurry to Socrates and throw their arms round him.*
PAUSANIAS *also climbs up and approaches Socrates with out-
stretched hand*]

PAUSANIAS I shall never understand democracy. If they want to kill you
why do they let you talk till you talk yourself clear out of it?

SOCRATES [*Taking his hand*] At least I'm left in possession of the field!

PAUSANIAS You had them out of their depth and you had me out of my
depth and maybe the same was true of the judge and the
jury. . . .

MAGIS.   If you will send up your ballots as rapidly as possible, mem-
bers of the jury! It will take only a few moments!
[*The lights dim down and go out for a little, to indicate a lapse
of time. When they come up they show the magistrate in the
center of the stage, a piece of paper in his hand. He studies the
paper slowly*]
The outcome of the trial—if you will be quiet for a moment—
the total vote stands at—if you will be quiet and listen—
the vote stands at—let me make sure of this—at 279 for
conviction and 221 for acquittal.

[*A light comes up on the edge of the stage and* XANTIPPE *is seen
to rise, crying a single choked word.* LAMPROCLES *rises and
puts his arm round her*]

XANTIPPE No!

LAMPROC. Mother!

[XANTIPPE *sits and is quiet. The light comes up on Socrates who
has heard the figures and comes to the center of the steps*]

SOCRATES I think you said—279 for conviction?

MAGIS.   I did, Socrates.

SOCRATES Then I'm found guilty.

MAGIS. It seems so.

SOCRATES Why, the jury which has been silent throughout has been thinking in its silence. And the outcome depends on the silent jury, not on us who were talking. I thought it would go the other way.

MAGIS. I thought so, too.

SOCRATES I thought it had gone the other way.
[*He looks slowly round at the crowd*]
I have not known my city then. More than half of these faces that look up at me are the faces of men who have said, "No more for Socrates." I've lived too long, perhaps, and you grow tired of me. Well, it's your right to grow weary of any man.

[ANYTAS *and* MELETOS *come running back*]

ANYTAS He's guilty?

MELETOS Guilty? Yes?

MAGIS. He's guilty. Satyros will take him into custody.

ANYTAS But he's about to speak again!

[SATYROS *climbs up and approaches Socrates*]

MAGIS. Yes. [*To Socrates*] It is now your privilege to propose an alternate punishment. The indictment asks for the death penalty.

SOCRATES Thank you, sir. I shall speak to that presently. But, first, let me tell the citizens of something that just begins to dawn on me. My accusers think, no doubt, that my death would be a great victory for them and a calamity for Socrates. This is not the case. My death would be of enormous benefit to me, but a disaster to my accusers . . . and to Athens. Look at what you will have done if this verdict stands. You will have laid hands on an ancient, flea-bitten, philosophic scamp, getting toward the end of his days, and made him into a great man. I have been called Socrates the Wise in mockery sometimes. But if this judgment is carried out I shall be called Socrates the Wise in earnest. I shall be famous, and my accusers will be infamous for all time! Look at this present you make me! I am old, seventy years old; I have lived a full life, I have done my work and said my say; and if you were to let me die quietly in bed I should be quietly forgotten. But a martyr's death sends a man off in a blaze of excitement and a blare of argument! Has a man of seventy ever before been offered martyrdom and the glory that goes with it? What could happen to me if I were to live out my life except the failure of powers which comes to brain and body in old age? And so for me this death would be great good fortune, but I cannot welcome it because in just so much as it brightens my name it blackens the name of Athens. And quite simply and honestly, citizens, I love Athens more than myself. Though this sentence means only good fortune to me it means evil fortune to my city, and I plead with you: Do not do this: Reverse your judgment: Let me die the unknown death I deserve! The alternate punishment I propose is that you fine me one mina—or thirty minae, or some such nominal sum—and maintain me henceforth at the public charge as a man serviceable to the state. That way I shall pass unnoticed into oblivion, and Athens will keep her good name.

ANYTAS   A fine! Oh, now we have him! Now we have him!

MAGIS.   This light sentence will never be accepted, Socrates. I must put it to the vote if you insist, but you will lose adherents and not gain them.

SOCRATES Nevertheless, this is truly what I think is due me from Athens. I cannot be dishonest about it.

LYCON   You insult your accusers!

SOCRATES No, Lycon, but I try to keep the issue clear. Those who wish me to live believe in the life of thought; those who wish me to die believe that men should do as they are told, without thinking. Those who wish me to live believe that every man should judge his own actions and those of his leaders; those who wish me to die believe that only the leaders should judge —and that even the leaders should think only what their fathers thought. And so I ask that the alternate sentence be a light fine. But please remember, citizens, when you vote, that it is my good luck to be tried in a democracy, where injustice, when it happens, is public and infrequent and therefore a cause for protest and astonishment. Under Critias there were thousands of political executions. If I had died under Critias nobody would have heard of me. In a despotism injustice is the usual thing and public opinion is not free to raise an outcry. But here in Athens my death would be first a nine-days' wonder, then a matter for controversy and recrimination—and then, in the end, if I am lucky in my friends and my times, my name and thoughts will last as long as our city's history! Truly, I do not wish my city dishonored to do me honor. And now—

[*He turns to the magistrate*]

MAGIS.   I must say again, Socrates, that if you give the jury no other choice the vote will go against you as before, or even more heavily against you.

SOCRATES Why, in that case, sir, who at seventy,
[*He turns to Satyros*]
who at seventy ever looked on a more beautiful visage than the face of this sad and ugly slave who brings men death?

[*The lights dim*]

END OF SCENE

Act Two

SCENE: *The scene is Socrates' cell before dawn some weeks later. Socrates lies asleep on a pallet on the floor. His legs are chained. Xantippe kneels beside him, waiting for him to wake. Phoenix leans against her knee. Lamprocles and Lysis stand waiting in the background.*

PHOENIX   [*Whispering*] Why is he to die today?

XANTIPPE   Hush! Don't wake him!
[*She turns to the older boys*]
He smiled in his sleep. He must be having good dreams.

LYSIS   I wonder if he ever had bad ones

LAMPROC.   I doubt it.

[SOCRATES *turns and opens his eyes*]

SOCRATES   What a strange dream!
[*He sits up*]
I thought a woman came to me, tall and fair and smiling, and she called, "Socrates! Socrates! In three days' time you will come to the fertile land of Phthia!" She was some kind of messenger, and she was pleased to bring the message and I was pleased to receive it.

XANTIPPE   We watched you smiling in your sleep.

SOCRATES   Have you just come, Xantippe?

XANTIPPE   No, we've been here some little time. We didn't like to wake you.

SOCRATES   Is it dark outside?

XANTIPPE   Yes, it's an hour or so before dawn.

SOCRATES   Still, you should have waked me. Why did you come early? Was there a reason?

XANTIPPE   Yes.

SOCRATES   The ship has come from Delos?

XANTIPPE   Yes. At least it had reached Sunium last night, and word of it came overland.

SOCRATES   It should cast anchor today then.

PHOENIX   Why does the ship matter?

SOCRATES   It's a sacred ship, Phoenix, dedicated to Apollo. Every year at this time it makes a voyage to the shrine of the god, and while it goes and returns no criminal can be executed in Athens. It happened to set out during my trial and I've had a long stay of execution.
[*He rubs his legs above the chains*]
How did you manage to get into the prison so early?

XANTIPPE   Oh, Satyros knows us now. More than that, I think he's inclined to grant us any little favors we want.

SOCRATES   We'll have a few moments' time together, at least, before this last day begins. The trouble is, what does one talk about on a last day? It's not a time for banter, I suppose, and yet I don't want to get off the usual stupid apothegms about loving your mother and being good citizens. Lamprocles, you're going to be the head of the family—what shall we discuss?

LAMPROC.   I'm not going to admit for a moment that this is your last day.

SOCRATES   Then we can joke if we like. You still intend to be a soldier, Lamprocles?

LAMPROC.   Yes, sir.

SOCRATES   I'm not sure you're enough of a rascal to succeed at that.

LAMPROC.   I'm working on rascality. I listened to the trial very carefully.

SOCRATES   Yes, there were some lessons there. You don't mean there was rascality on my side?

LAMPROC.　You use it for your own purposes.

SOCRATES　As a matter of fact, I do. Yes, you might make a soldier. Lysis, are you still studying ticks?

LYSIS　No. That was a beetle, and not a tick. But I think geometry is the greatest thing in the world. You can measure anything by geometry!

SOCRATES　Can you measure the earth?

LYSIS　They say there's even a way to measure the earth now, by marking how the sun's rays fall, first in one city and then in another.

SOCRATES　By the time you grow up perhaps it won't be atheistic to say such things. But watch it for a few years.

LYSIS　I will.

SOCRATES　Phoenix, when you grow up and get married don't keep your wife penned up in the women's quarters. Let her out for a run once in a while.

PHOENIX　There won't be any women's quarters in my house. My wife will walk all over my house, anywhere she pleases.

SOCRATES　Good. There speaks the new generation. Of course occasionally you may be sorry. You may wish that there were at least men's quarters which she couldn't enter—but I'll let you settle that.

PHOENIX　Anyway, you're not going to die today.

SOCRATES　Who told you?

PHOENIX　Pausanias.

SOCRATES　Is Pausanias still here?

XANTIPPE　He came back. He came back, he says, to get you out of prison.

SOCRATES   Good old Stupid!

XANTIPPE   It was he who let us in early. He has influence with the guards.

SOCRATES   Influence is of many kinds, of course.

XANTIPPE   He has them all.

[*One of the thugs enters*]

SOCRATES   Satyros is up early, too. He has sent a harbinger.

XANTIPPE   It was he who let us in.

[*Another thug enters, followed by* SATYROS *and* PAUSANIAS. *Theodote lingers discreetly in the background*]

SOCRATES   Why, this is hardly a prison at all! Satyros, these shackles are somewhat numbing to the legs and feet. Welcome, Pausanias.

PAUSANIAS You won't wear them much longer, Socrates. Greetings. [*He starts toward Socrates, but is stopped by the thugs*] What's this?

SATYROS   We do a cash business here.

PAUSANIAS The money? I think my credit should be good.

SATYROS   Nobody's credit is good here.

PAUSANIAS I am the king of Sparta, you horrible clown.

SATYROS   There are no kings here, Stupid.

PAUSANIAS I'm not called Stupid by everybody, Satyros.

SATYROS   In Athens you are. In Athens anybody can call anybody anything.

PAUSANIAS More democracy. Well, how do I know you'll let him out?

SATYROS   How do I know I'll be paid?

PAUSANIAS [*Producing a sack*] Take it. Three hundred silver owls.
[SATYROS *takes the sack and starts out*]
Where are you going?

SATYROS   To count it.

PAUSANIAS Take off the leg irons first.

SATYROS   [*To his thugs*] Take them off.
[*The thugs unlock the shackles and remove them*]
The children should not be here.

[SATYROS *goes out*]

THEODOTE I'll take them out. Lysis, Phoenix.

[*She takes the two younger boys by the hand and goes out with
them.* LAMPROCLES *follows*]

SOCRATES Forgive me for not rising. My legs don't serve me at the
moment. What are you buying from Satyros?

PAUSANIAS Socrates, when I went back to Sparta I found myself restless
and dissatisfied. The occupations of a Spartan king are hunting, making war, and dispensing justice in the courts. I went
out as usual and killed some animals; I made an expedition
and reduced a small city—very profitable this was—and I
sat as judge for a while. Nothing was satisfactory. I moped
about the palace. I had the sensation of homesickness, of
having lost what made life worth living. And when I went
over it in my stupid brain it came down to this—I missed my
Socrates and I missed my Theodote. I came back to get them.

[THEODOTE *returns*]

SOCRATES And Theodote is complaisant?

THEODOTE I will go.

SOCRATES And Satyros will sell me?

PAUSANIAS Glad to do it. He likes you.

SOCRATES And Xantippe and the boys?

PAUSANIAS It's all arranged, and there's room for as many as you take with you. Xantippe wants a palace. Well, she shall have it. It's cold, and it looks more like a barn, but it's what's called a palace. It's yours.

SOCRATES What a wonderful offer!

XANTIPPE And he offers you an income, Socrates.

SOCRATES I'm to be a man of means!
[*He rubs his legs*]
What a singular relation pleasure has to pain! The shackles were painful on my legs, and now the pain is gone and I feel great pleasure in its place.

PAUSANIAS Also you've been poor all your life and now you're to be a rich man. It ought to work the same way.

XANTIPPE It does.

SOCRATES Xantippe, when a woman buys a fish in the market does she look at it before she pays?

XANTIPPE Now he's going to say we must examine into this offer.

SOCRATES Shouldn't we?

XANTIPPE You're being offered life in place of death!

SOCRATES Well, a life is more important than a fish, Xantippe. And it's not only I who should examine what I am to receive. The king should examine me before he buys me from Satyros, for it may be that he won't like what he's getting.

PAUSANIAS I know what I'm getting. I'm getting Socrates.

SOCRATES But now remember what Socrates is. He is an obnoxious old fellow without sandals, badly dressed, walking up and down the streets putting annoying questions to the inhabitants.

PAUSANIAS You won't have to go outside to talk, Socrates. You will sit in my palace with me and talk to me and my friends. None of this wandering about the streets.

SOCRATES But suppose I grew tired of talking with important people and wanted to have a chat with shoemakers or weavers or the athletes in the palaestra?

PAUSANIAS Hm.

SOCRATES What do you say?

PAUSANIAS Well, you know, this hadn't occurred to me, but it is a difficulty. Nobody goes about asking questions in Sparta. And if you asked them nobody would answer you.

SOCRATES Why not, O King?

PAUSANIAS They—they wouldn't be interested.

SOCRATES I might . . . at length, after a while . . . rouse some interest.

PAUSANIAS It wouldn't be encouraged. You'd do better just staying in the palace and talking there. You see, Sparta is not a democracy. We don't do things that way.

SOCRATES In other words I wouldn't be allowed to talk?

PAUSANIAS Not in the streets, no. But mind you, you might have a great deal of influence on me.

SOCRATES Do you mind if I call you Stupid?

PAUSANIAS From now on call me Stupid, nothing else.

SOCRATES This is how it stands, Stupid. If the judge and the jury had told me they'd let me off if I'd stay at home and quit my question-and-answer game, I'd have said "Proceed, gentlemen; I'll live as I've always lived, and if that's incompatible with the laws why put me out of the way." In Sparta, as in Athens, I must wrangle and make inquiries in my accustomed fashion. Otherwise I prefer the hemlock. I'm old and set in my ways.

XANTIPPE Socrates, we have three children. When a man has children hasn't he some responsibility to bring them up and train them?

SOCRATES Yes. I don't like to leave you.

XANTIPPE Surely there's a city somewhere on the Mediterranean where a man can speak his mind. In Ionia, or Sicily, or farther west.

SOCRATES Is there such a one, Stupid?

PAUSANIAS I'm trying to think. . . . No, Athens is the only democracy. The others are despotisms—of one or of many. It's a pretty realistic world in the main. Several cities have tried democracy off and on, but it didn't work, it never does, and they got sick of it, and some enlightened strong man always took over.

SOCRATES You mean that east and west, north and south, all round the Mediterranean, Athens is the one democracy?

PAUSANIAS As far as I know. Men need discipline, Socrates, and they like it, too. And they come back to it.

SOCRATES Would I be subject to discipline if I went with Xantippe to Sparta?

PAUSANIAS Not a bit of it. What kind of discipline would I use on you?

SOCRATES Suppose you took a dislike to me? Suppose I were found out in the road, colloquing with villagers?

PAUSANIAS Look, you dizzy old goat, you'd get your neck twisted, that's all.

XANTIPPE [*Anguished*] Socrates—I see a little streak of gray in the sky! In a few moments they will all be here and Satyros won't be able to let you through. You're all we have! You're all we'll ever have! The king would never hurt you. He just says these things when you corner him. It's now or not at all,

Socrates! Maybe it doesn't matter so much to you, maybe you can bear it, but think of us!

SOCRATES If I die here, Pausanias, will you take care of Xantippe?

PAUSANIAS Whether you come or stay she shall have her palace.

[SOCRATES *gets up and puts his arm round Xantippe*]

SOCRATES I have lived such a wonderful life, Xantippe, and you have, too. We have known the greatest men who ever lived on this earth; we knew Pericles and Aspasia and the masters of arts and words who built the Parthenon and filled the theater with music at the foot of the hill where it stands. We have lived as we pleased, thought what we pleased, said what we pleased. Shall I dwindle now into a king's buffoon, hanging to the ragged end of life by saying the right things and keeping Stupid amused?

XANTIPPE But you'd be alive!

SOCRATES Is that so important?

XANTIPPE Then I'll go! Stay and die if you insist. The children shall have their chance. I'll go!

SOCRATES Go if you must. If you think it's good for them. But I think they're better off in Athens.

XANTIPPE Athens is killing you!

SOCRATES They seek for justice here. They don't always find it but they seek it. They gave me a trial. Are there such trials in Sparta, Stupid?

PAUSANIAS We have trials. But we decide who's guilty before the court sits. We have that much sense.

[SATYROS *enters with the sack*]

SATYROS There are three hundred drachmas here, Stupid, but forty-seven of them are Corinthian or worse. I want that forty-seven in Athenian owls.

PAUSANIAS Later, then.

SATYROS   No, not later. Now.

PAUSANIAS How am I going to find you forty-seven of the right kind now?

SATYROS   You'll find them—or he doesn't live.

PAUSANIAS You know what happens to slaves who speak to me that way? They die!

SATYROS   Pinion him!
[*The two thugs swiftly twist the king's arms behind him*]
And don't talk about killing. You're breaking the law here. You offered me money to release a prisoner.

PAUSANIAS And you took it!

SATYROS   Prove that.

[*He tosses the sack of money to the floor*]

THEODOTE [*Coming forward*] I have fifty Athenian drachmas here, Satyros. Take them, add them to what you have and let us go.
[*She gives Satyros her purse*]
I wouldn't lie to you.

SATYROS   Lie? Of course you'd lie. Why not? But I'll take them. And now go. All of you.

XANTIPPE There's light in the sky.

SATYROS   It's not too late. There's a back way. But be quick about it.
[*To the thugs*] Let him go.

[*The thugs release Pausanias.* SATYROS *picks up the sack*]

SOCRATES You'd better give the money back, Satyros. I'm not leaving.

SATYROS   What trick is this?

SOCRATES No trick. I'm not escaping.

SATYROS   We made our bargain, and the money's changed hands. It's too late to make new terms.

SOCRATES   You don't take my meaning, Satyros. I'm remaining in the prison.

SATYROS   Why?

SOCRATES   I prefer it to Sparta.

SATYROS   The hemlock is prepared and ready. You're to drink it this morning. I have my orders.

SOCRATES   So we are to be together at the end, after all!

SATYROS   The woman shall have her money back.

SOCRATES   Why, good.

SATYROS   And the king may have his.

SOCRATES   Good.

SATYROS   [*Returning the money to Theodote and Pausanias*] And now go. You're free. It's a gift from Satyros to Socrates! Go!

SOCRATES   You've been a slave all your life, Satyros, and perhaps you won't understand this, but it's better to die than to live not free.

SATYROS   I don't . . . understand it. I don't want to give you the hemlock.

SOCRATES   You won't need to give it to me. Just bring it and I'll drink it.

PAUSANIAS Shall we remain while you drink it?

SOCRATES   I think you should go.

THEODOTE   Crito and Phaedo are here.

          [CRITO *and* PHAEDO *enter at the rear*]

SOCRATES I'll converse with them over the cup.

XANTIPPE Oh, Socrates!

SOCRATES Yes—

XANTIPPE If you drink it—this is the last time—for your friends, and for you and for me!

SOCRATES Maybe there's no good way, Xantippe, but I think this comes as close as there is to being a good way. Go now with Pausanias. You and Theodote.

XANTIPPE Do you have . . . no last word for me?

SOCRATES Do you think we can better now what we have given each other over all these years?

PAUSANIAS [*To Xantippe*] Come.

XANTIPPE Then I have a last word for you. I shall not go to Sparta. I shall live in our old house on the three obols a day.

SOCRATES You do this for the children?

XANTIPPE No, for you. I can remember you there. It's the only way I can keep you. Any of you. Will you be with me there sometimes?

SOCRATES Perhaps I shall not be there or anywhere, Xantippe. Nowhere at all.

XANTIPPE But in spirit—if I could have your spirit with me—

SOCRATES My spirit you can certainly have, and anyone can have it who remembers it and wants it.

XANTIPPE Yes. You escape me now as before.

SOCRATES We all escape when we die, Xantippe. From everybody. But you will live in the old house on the three obols?

XANTIPPE Yes.

SOCRATES Then—
[*He goes close to her*]
Will you sometimes say my prayer for me?

XANTIPPE If I remember it.

SOCRATES [*Putting his arm round her*] Say it now, and I'll prompt you
if you forget, and then you'll have it all.

XANTIPPE Now?

SOCRATES Yes, now.

XANTIPPE "Beloved Pan, and all you other gods who haunt this city"—
oh, no, no, no! I can't lose you! I can't live!

SOCRATES Go on, Xantippe. "Give me beauty in the inward soul"—

XANTIPPE "Give me beauty in the inward soul"—

SOCRATES "For outward beauty I'm not likely to have"—

XANTIPPE "For outward beauty I'm not likely to have"—

[*The lights begin to dim down and during the next speeches go
out entirely*]

SOCRATES "May I reckon the wise to be the wealthy"—

XANTIPPE I know the rest. "May I reckon the wise to be the wealthy
and those who need least to be most like the gods."

[*The lights are out*]

SOCRATES "And those who need least to be most like the gods."

CURTAIN